لا شيء ثابت...كل شيء مباح

For the Children of Baphomet

The Book of Baphomet

Nikki Wyrd
and
Julian Vayne

Copyright © 2012 Mandrake, Julian Vayne, Nikki Wyrd

First edition

All rights reserved. No part of this work may be reproduced or utilized in any form by any means electronic or mechanical, including *xerography, photocopying, microfilm*, and *recording*, or by any information storage system without permission in writing from the publishers.

Also available by Julian Vayne:
Now That's What I Call Chaos Magick (with Greg Humphries)
Pharmakon
Magick Works

Contents

Invocation 11

The Song of Life 13

Evolution 29

Elucidation 32

First Contact 34

Out of the Eastern Temple 40

Fire Underground 48

The Magical Conspiracy 58

The Inheritors of Baphomet 63

Enlightenment 74

Of Caves and Spires 80

Age old wisdom 83

Deep ecology 85

That Discordian Conspiracy so far… 94

Licking Baphomet into Shape 96

Satanic orgy shocker! 106

Stars in their eyes 112

Goddess 115

The Tell-Tale Head 118

Enter the Horned God 120

Not with a Bang 130

Serpent Dance 135

Embrace the Chaos 139

The Will to Live 145

The Death of Baphomet 149

Chains of Life after Death 159

Dredd Lord of the Shadows 161

Alchemy 170

Baphomet Revisioned 174

Toad in the hole, Whole in the Toad 179

Deep Baphomet 186

Stories from The Circle of Baphomet 188

Horns of Baphomet yoga 195

Gnostic Chaosphere Ritual 197

Baphomet Through the Spheres 204

Valediction 223

Artworks

Fig 1 -   Astaroth, prince of Hell, from J.A.S. Collin de Plancy, *Dictionnaire Infernal*. Original illustration by *Louis Breton*, engraved by M. Jarrault.

Fig 2 -   Baphomet, from Eliphas Levi's *Dogme et Rituel de la Haute Magie*.

Fig 3 -   *L'Azoth des Philosophes*, Basil Valentine, 1659.

Fig 4 -   Alchemical Seal reproduced in Stanislas Klossowski de Rola *The Golden Game: Alchemical Engravings of the Seventeenth Century*.

Fig 5 -   Advertising for *Les Mystères de la franc-maçonnerie dévoilés* by Léo Taxil.

Fig 6 -   Advertising for *Les Mystères de la franc-maçonnerie dévoilés* by Léo Taxil.

Fig 7 -   Baphomet at a Freemason session from the work of Léo Taxil.

Fig 8 -   Goat's head pentagram from *La Clef de la Magie Noire* by Stanislas de Guaita.

Fig 9 -   Detail of a stele of King Melishipak I (1186–1172 BC), showing a version of the ancient Mesopotamian eight-pointed star symbol of the goddess Ishtar. Excavated by Jacques de Morgan photograph by Marie-Lan Nguyen.

Fig 10 - Baphomet by Frater Tadhg.

Fig 11 -   Julian Vayne as Baphomet in Trafalgar Square as part of Antony Gormley's installation One and Other. Photograph by Simon Costin, 2009.

Fig 12 -   The Eyes of the Day, photograph by Nikki Wyrd.

Fig 13 -   Symbols of the Gnostic Chaosphere Rite by Frater Tadhg.

Fig 14 -   Baphomet by Frater Fux.

Fig 15 -   Baphomet by Lee Noble.

Acknowledgments

Frater Pelagius, for comments & support throughout this process. Frater Stokastikos, for allowing us to reprint the material from Arcanorium College, and telling us tales of his history. Frater Tadhg, for his skilful assistance with the cover, limited edition print and other artworks in this volume. To Frater Fux, and Lee Noble, for permission to reproduce their conceptualisations of Baphomet. Thanks to our draft readers; Ronald Hutton, Levannah Morgan, Alistair Livingston, Ian Read and Peter J. Carroll.

Thanks

From Nikki: Thanks to the vast community of the interweb, many of whom I shall never know as individuals, for spreading stuff around. Thank you to all those chaos magicians I have known and loved. Thanks to my children for understanding me (some of the time!) and for putting up with me incessantly tapping away at a keyboard. Most of all, thanks to my co-author, with whom I have shared ecstasy of spirit, and joy on earth.

From Julian: Thanks to all those wonderful people who support and inspire me. Thank you to all those contributors to the network of minds that is the internet. Thank you to my children, you who are the new eyes of Baphomet, may you see a future of pleasure and freedom and power.

Baphomet - give me the sign of the Open Eye:
Octarine rays shine
Double coiled, star formed snake, time travelling
Four-fold alphabet of ecstasy.
You are the Tree, and the Snake.
We are the children of the Trees, embedded actions
You raise us toward the sun and the moon, greatest of all gods
Unfolding, opening, pouring forth upon the world
with torrents of fire
Cell of undifferentiated possibility,
such beauty, awe full to behold
All devourer, all begetter, Winged angel of Life
Male and female conjoined. I see myself, O my god
In your serpentine dance I see you, O my god
Ancient, New, Deep Space. You rest.
Your language speaks from star and stone,
Loving to the very heart of the Earth
You make a road for the Spirit to pass over.
Waving the wand
Drumming pulse of creation and obliteration, breathing easily
Wide awake to the world Begetter
All paths lead to your hearth, touching hands
Root of all things fresh as the day it was born
Bringer of death and decay, sleep and birth and love growing perfection,
Branches made of air point to the sky
All pervading desire Opening as Love...
Transformer and Transgressor Doing magick
Axis of sky and land and sea in every blade of grass,
every day's eye.
Weaver of magick. Folded legs
Forked lightning that quickens all matter,
creating laughter anew!

The Song of Life

The Stars are but thistles in that waste, pregnant seed heads that burst, releasing their strange cargo into vast space. From the heart of the stars, drifting outward from supernovae and the dull trails of brown dwarves, emerge the elements. Forged in the fusion fires of titanic nuclear furnaces, as the ancient stars dwindle expand and explode, they scatter new matter through the cosmos. From this nucleosynthesis hydrogen begets helium, helium begets carbon, carbon begets oxygen. Stars a little more massive than our sun form iron cores by this process. Heavier elements are a job for flaming orbs orders of magnitude bigger, where gold and lead are liberated from the alchemy of the supernova and smeared across the sky in thunderous detonation.

Such is the stuff that we are made of. From whale to woodlouse, our bodies quite literally come from the core of the stars.

The vast particulate pentacle from which our earth was made was once a cloud of such star-stuff. The cloud thickened, gathered, and the central portion of this disk (which was at first over 3 light years in diameter) folded up, dense and hot. Gravity, that love of mass for mass, pulled the centre tighter together until it ignited. Our sun turned on.

The negative entropy from that event, this new massive body at the heart of the swirling cloud, began to organise the rest. Less massive regions of stellar dust coalesced; some almost became large enough to ignite, which would have produced a binary star system. But in the end Jupiter couldn't get it together to become another sun. The rest settled down to condense and cool. The planets formed.

The Earth was new

In the tumult of the new solar system a planet, perhaps as large as Mars, collided with our world. This chance blow set the Earth spinning; it was this act of great violence that gave us the axis mundi and our world's eccentric 23 degree inclination to the ecliptic. The giant impact distorted early Earth into a wobbling egg of molten fire. The core of the impactor spiralled down and was absorbed into the heart of early Earth. Rocky fragments from the blast careered into space, conglomerated and became, perhaps in as a little as a year, our moon.

Still shedding heat from its creation, the depths of our planet thrashed around like angry dragons. Volcanic eruptions were frequent. The wild spinning of the world (each rotation lasted six hours) caused rapid changes in temperature. The newly acquired moon was much nearer, a vast orb capable of pulling the tides hundreds of feet into the air. As the gravitational pull of our satellite swept round the earth its strength was sufficient to ripple the rocks of the newly solid crust, pulling them, plastic and pliant, upwards.

Some of the water had perhaps arrived as comets but whatever its origin the earth, as it cooled, was now covered with a turbulent sea. Islands with volcanic tips peeped above the waterline belching sulphurous fumes into the atmosphere. This is a red world. Smog clouds the skies, orange tinged with methane green; these clouds are reflected in the red water in which iron is dissolved. Meteors still strike the surface of this world, although the 'Late Heavy Bombardment' is mercifully over. Perhaps it is riding on these wandering shooting stars that life arrives from a cosmic panspermia: If so, that simply pushes the nativity of organic systems away from our world to another distant planet, perhaps one with much the same conditions as our own.

Now the extraterrestrial actors were all assembled. Players ready to perform their parts. Within those molten seas the aeons-old elements made from the heart of long-forgotten stars waited. All that was needed was an easy source of energy. Life is implicit in chemistry, as geometry is in mathematics. There need be no outside god, no prime mover on the darkness of the depths. 13.7 billion years after the universe appears to have begun, 4.5 billion years ago our earth began to form and 3.9 billion years ago the chemistry of life began to wake up. This was not life based on the energy of the sun but rather in the arcane depths of the oceans. Life began in Atlantis.

Once upon a time, cellular life began. The most likely place for this lurks beneath the waves, around one of those hydrothermal vents we now describe as an extreme environment. Within the deposited minerals, bubbles in the rock exist that are just the right size for the rich soup of organic chemistry to form itself into the internal components of a system of self replicating cells.

All it took was the arrival of nice costumes to wear, and the cell contents could move out of their green room onto the stage of the big wide world...

The wild primordial sea contains some very special zones. Places where the slow movement of the earth's crust create new seabed from the planet's mantle. Rather than the more violent regions of buckling and subduction (from which rise up the jagged teeth of new mountains), these are comparatively gentle areas driven by tectonic power. These places are a species of hydrothermal vent, but they are not the vigorous 'black smokers', rapidly crumbling and re-forming towers spewing boiling metal sulphides into the sea. Instead these more sedate formations are generated as freshly exposed rocks from the mantle react with seawater. The water bubbles through the fresh rock and becomes one with it. Intricate, complex hydroxide minerals are created, these vents produce the rock we call serpentine. With its markings like scales, the signature of life has a stone snake at its heart.

As the rock and seawater intertwine, the rock fractures, bubbles, breaks. More water can now react with deeper surfaces of the mantle. Gradually these water soaked rocks are pulled down into the deep fiery earth. In this way water is pumped down into the superheated depths of the planet, driving the convection currents in the magma of our world. The union of water and fire churns up the seas and maintains the rhythmic disequilibria of the whole earth.

Heat is also released by this reaction, gentle warmth in comparison with the 400 degrees centigrade of your average black smoker vent. A primal alchemist, the serpentine vents' chemistry splits the seawater, liberating hydrogen as well as heat and creating a redox cloud of elements; carbon dioxide, methane, nitrogen, ammonia – scavenged from the trace elements in seawater. If you want your creation to start with a cauldron of primeval soup then here it is.

As these chemicals and heat burst upwards from the rock they spread out over the fresh ocean floor that is rising up from the mantle. As they grow the bubbling gasses create a lattice of tiny chambers within the rock. These are alkaline palaces of carbonates, ice white towers rising from the seabed. There is no smoke apparent from the filigree chimneys of these rocks, their emissions are colourless. But year on year these citadels build themselves, reaching heights in excess of sixty metres, and the activity at such vents can last for tens of thousands of years. And it is in this honeycomb of microscopic tubes and cells that life first began.

It all started with alchemy. The mixture of molecules and spheres of rock creating bubbles separate from their environment. The first magick circles.

These rooms, separated from each other with thin aragonite walls, are where life builds itself. Held in these tiny vessels the basic chemical reactions that underpin all metabolism on our world could begin. Hydrogen gas seeping up from the rocks, a rare source of free energy in our world, was captured and became incorporated into chemical reactions that are spontaneous and inevitable. Gradually the vent chambers grew, tens of thousands of spaces cycling the reactions which would give rise to organic molecules, to long polymers. The ouroboros of chemistry deposited longer and longer molecules in those miniscule wombs. Some would squeeze into the cells nearby, pumped about by the warm water circulating through the chalky citadels. Others would lurk, motionless in their chambers, coiling and re-coiling. Chemical reactions proliferated in complexity. The intricate reaction known as the citric acid or Krebs cycle emerges from these gyrating permutations. This is the key reaction of biology, a great worm of chemistry encircling the base of the tree of life, essential to both aerobic and anaerobic organisms. Essential to cells that are simple and those that are complex. Swirling away in those tiny chambers, driven by the free lunch of hydrogen and comforted by the chemically diverse yet physically secure environment of the serpentine vents, this reaction became the core around which more elaborate processes developed. The cascade of chemiosmosis, the flow of ions across the membranes of these ancient proto-cells gives rise to Adenosine-5'-triphosphate (ATP) the fundamental unit of energy which all life requires. Fed by ATP the citric acid serpent spins, generating the essential components of biology. Chemistry is what we were and are.

As ATP accumulated, the Kreb cycle was able to generate a bewildering range of molecules. Long polymer snakes arose in increasing complexity until, in those warm hideaways, a molecule formed that could not only produce proteins but could evolve, in the biological sense, by encoding information and being acted upon by natural selection. Our primordial snake now has memory, coded into pairs of amino acids. RNA appeared first, a freeform beat poet making it up on the spot, sometimes turning out dross, other times golden lines much in demand. It took the reliable memory of DNA, the prompter of our drama, to start the negative entropy escalation away from total Chaos towards the start of a greater order.

Our actors are on stage and have their lines ready; reading off the sequence of DNA by RNA constitutes the play. The script is spoken; the pairs of bases reproduce, mutate and drift, mixing the letters A, G, T, C into a code. These codes form words, phrases, sentences and eventually a whole language of chemical structure. Each sequence defines the emergence of amino acids and thus proteins. Proteins fold up into structures, they are the enzymes that catalyse further complex reactions, they act as glue, sticking together structures that have arisen in the proto-cell. They carry data, signals of knowledge. They formulate the anatomy and function of all that lives.

Under hundreds of metres of sea these wheels within wheels of chemical ingenuity thrive. Fed by the interaction of oceanic water and fiery rocks. The hatchery of the serpentine vents contain this microcosm of what is to come. Chemical cycles, what we call 'life' emerges, to thrive, interact and persist. This process, darkly hidden in the belly of the sea, is where we come from. In all the billions of years that have passed these processes remain unchanged. The world of men and of these arcane life forms is rooted in identical nests of chemical consequences. As unavoidable as gravity, life begins for no other reason than it must.

Thus the inevitable and variable code of life came into being. Far above the surface of our world the 'second atmosphere' cocooned the planet. Carbon dioxide, nitrogen and water vapour occluded the sun rendering its light pale and yellow. Deep under the sea life was still attached to the umbilical cord of the serpentine vents but this was to change. The roulette of natural selection fell favourably for one group of cells that were able to move. The serpentine vents in the ancient oceans would, eventually, fail. Choked and dying, cut off from their nourishing hydrogen, some of cells discovered ways of creating their own cell walls from hydrophobic lipids. These organically produced capsules allowed those intrepid adventurers to set sail through the primordial ocean, seeds cast out, seeking for new vents upon which they might fall and set up home. Sometimes these cells would find themselves arriving in places where nourishment for their chemical cycles could be drawn from the rocks in which they lodged. For some these habitats were ones in shallow seas. Alternately exposed and submerged, as the gigantic moon swept around in her orbit, sometimes food was scarce. These early creatures were left high and dry and hungry. But these cells possessed, implicit in their chemistry, the potential to produce intricate machinery that might use light particles to initiate the production of chemical energy. While continuing to lunch on hydrogen sulphide from volcanic vents they began to generate their own organic matter from atmospheric carbon dioxide.

As the sea level dropped around these colonies of cyanobacteria so they would switch on a backup form of photosynthesis to nourish themselves. Harvesting the light of the Precambrian sun they could continue to make ATP, unable to grow but still alive, they would wait until the richness of the hydrothermal vent became available once more. But what if the vent never returned? The levels of ultraviolet radiation reaching the surface of earth during those days were far in excess of what we know today. Unchecked, the light powered photosynthesis would have damaged the cells with electrons bouncing around, wreaking havoc on the ancient DNA code. The solution seems to have come from crystals. Manganese was common in the ancient oceans and crystals of this metal, interjected within the primitive photosynthetic language of the cyanobacteria prevented cellular damage. How such a crystal became wedged into the system is unknown, perhaps the collapse of a cliff hurling debris wildly about or some more mysterious process. But however it happened, charged by the sun's rays, these tiny crystals allowed those organisms to split water into hydrogen and oxygen. The crystalline jewels became incorporated into the cells, clasped in the protein settings of a new life form. Free from the hydrothermal vents new pillars of life, the stromatolites, squatting in the warm shallows, began to change our world. For the first time the chemical process we call life would remake the composition of the atmosphere, spewing out a gas that would protect later generations from the harsh ultraviolet radiation. This gas, over millions of years, poured into the sky. The chloroplasts in the stromatolites flourished, a blue atmosphere and green earth had begun. Life breathed oxygen into the heavens.

Thus began the green world. A world of slimes, of moulds, of films of living ooze that stretched across the planet. Each cell duplicates its nest of whirling chemical reactions. Encoded in the twin spiralled serpent of DNA, written out copy after copy, the clone green fingers of biology spread into every crevice of the rock, the ocean, the atmosphere. Biology was a slow verdant hum of replicating organic crystals. Life was like this for 3 billion years: growing and fermenting. Some cells gathered together in colonies to form larger systems, what today we call 'creatures'. They fashioned feathery fractal bodies deep in the sea. A bold experiment, these paper thick fern-shaped beings swayed in the lightless water for several million years. And then the climate altered (perhaps an unwitting change instigated by photosynthesising life itself?). Snow began to fall until it invaded even the tropics. At the poles the ice was over a kilometre think. The photosynthesising bacteria changed some of their chemistry to cope, but the gas feeding fractal ferns in the oceans folded up origami style, and died.

After a few million years, the thaw came and the ice began to melt. The bold sun fell again on the land, which, sculpted by glacial grinding, flushed a fecund dust of minerals into the seas. The green organisms bloomed far out over the warming ocean. All was alive in this second Eden. Then our serpent DNA plays another trick. Another coil unwinds in the delicious mathematics of possibility. Some cells began eating their companions. Morphing bodies flow around smaller forms; microcosm engulfed microcosm. In these predations certain bacteria were assimilated by their larger cousins. Rather being consumed these cells were incorporated whole and alive into their hosts. The mitochondrial cell became encased in another life form, which erected a hall of polymerised molecules to house its new treasure. As these complex cells, the eukaryotes, spread through the world they would carry with them the stench of sex.

Sex is the amphetamine of evolution. A handy way of shaking all your chromosomes about and getting variation both faster and in a way that is likely to favour the previous set of variations that worked best. It's a biological epic win and has swept through life on this planet like a dose of the pox. As soon as complex cells had started fucking the whole system goes into overdrive. Within an evolutionary eyeblink we have multi-cellular animals; long tube creatures filtering for food in marshy rivers. Such animals possessed segmented bodies and highly specialised cells. The eukaryotes that comprised them, born of sexual fusion, carried instructions not only for the single cell but also for how the cell would relate to its neighbours. The protein collagen was manufactured by these creatures to lock them into place. The shape of life, previously extending in little more than two dimensions, could become seriously 3D. Life was solid and with solidity came mobility. This revolution happened on the backs of the green plants. They'd sculpted the atmosphere to a state where it was now heavy with oxygen. This gas was to ignite metabolic furnaces which forged the great changes that were to come.

Disk shaped animals, Dickinsonia, like animated marine pizzas, etched their way across this ancient sea. Vanguard of the 'Cambrian explosion' (the shamelessly quick emergence of complex animals) beasts like Dickinsonia stuttered their way across submerged rocks. Chemical bonds forming and snapping and reforming, created the beginning of the muscular systems employed by millions of multi-celled creatures. And as it moved this magical disk would graze. Scraping the green slime from the stone, this moving predator, child of sex and death began the dance of the hunter and the hunted.

Strategy. Complex adaptation has entered the game. Evolution, like some devilish genius player of Mornington Crescent, adopted new and complex rules, process heaped upon process, guess upon second guess. We were all using the bus routes to get to Kings Cross now.

As sex and death turned up the heat, so the three-dimensional body form stabilised. The mad experiments of the early Cambrian yielded to the tried and trusted format; bi-lateral symmetry. Head (ideal location for sensory organs), body (segmented with the potential to grow specialised segments or 'limbs'), tail (featuring anus). 'Central gut' was popular, as was 'long' rather than 'wide'. The world had suddenly become a space. Animals could move. No longer was sexual reproduction limited to the chance dalliance of ovum with sperm released, free floating, into the ocean (their tryst determined by rhythm of the moon). Instead fucking could happen anytime when two or more creatures met and the atmosphere was right. The hunger of cunt for cock had begun.

With evolution all awhirl you needed to keep your head. In fact it was essential to get your sex cells to code for more and more fine-tuned senses in your multi-celled form. Keeping up with the data stream, especially now that 3D space was involved, was a pressing need. No longer were approaches such as simple absorption (smell) the sole order of the day. Methods for knowledge at a distance were required. One might opt for specialised cells that detected vibration (sound), that responded to pressure (touch) or, following the lead of grandmother chloroplast, why not use light? Early adopters like the trilobites alpha tested eyes right from ground zero of the Cambrian explosion. They were hooked on these optical gizmos and hung onto them for over 300 million years. Plated tanks for bodies, their eyes were calcite crystals. Improbable diamonds crowning its head, the trilobite was the first observer of nature. Different collections of cells approached sight in different ways. In some creatures one of the ribs of DNA itself, guanine, was used. We can still see it flash as the organic crystalline reflection of a cat's eye or fish's scale. Crystals, being at the border of organic and inorganic chemistry (if such a distinction really means anything) and having uniform optical properties, were the most common way for cells to learn to see. The proteins of the vertebrate lens, known as crystallins, continue the trilobites' ground-breaking style.

Reaction to this new world of sight, of sound, of enhanced mobility, bootstrapped the cycles of cells into previously unseen levels of awareness. Cells begin to specialise in intricately connected networks not only to interact with the world but to perceive the world by developing awareness. Representations are formed by connections in cells we know as nerves. A sense of location in space, the presence or absence of food, of predators, or threats, develop. The world is reborn through the chemical impulses and electrical gradients. The world becomes know as an apparently separate 'thing', symbolic representations arise that mimic reality through the perceptual net. In the head part and, languidly distributed throughout the whole body, webs of chemical interactions give rise to brains and their accompanying epiphenomena, minds. Parts of the territory have grown their own maps, with customised layers of relevant information.

And within these brains sensory input and internal mentation becomes something felt, something experienced. The seed crystal of an 'I' develops which can 'have' feelings. These first thoughts, formed in the ooze of the ancient oceans, are the foundation upon which all consciousness is built.

As the seas seethe with moving, eating, fucking things, so they begin to emerge onto land. Where first only mats of organic green covered the surface soon the forms of animals are to be seen. Sparkling eyes pop up above the waterline and watch the stars.

Rushing outward, life pours variation, focused through the lenses of adaptation, mutation and sexual reproduction, upon form. The slow conquest of dimension allows some groups of cells to call forth fins, and legs, tentacles and tails. By the Silurian period wings sprout where once were only cilia. The first creatures to fly were the insects and the first of them probably did so to enter a space where mating could take place. The challenge of emerging from the waters, a dizzy and untried nymph, to get airborne. This test of fitness was a sharp evolutionary spur. Flies fucked in the humid air. The skies of earth buzzed and throbbed to the sound of dragonflies bigger than crows.

Cellular plans are re-drawn. Eggs, once squishy things, corral minerals to develop harder shells. They can now leave the oceans warm embrace and breed in the air. Like little balloons of seawater, sealed in skins and scales, larger and larger beings inhabit the earth. At sea bony plates cover fishes. The emergence of sight brings with it a profusion of colour. Creatures signal, advertise or lie about their edibility. They display to demonstrate the quality of the genetic payload they are carrying. The eater, arrayed in camouflage, sneaks up on the eaten.

The cells that have opted to stick with photosynthesis as their manna rise up and, following the complex non-linearity of chaos, sprout fern shaped leaves upon the earth. You really can't see the wood for the trees. Striking upwards the forest spreads across the earth.

After the trees came, the level of atmospheric oxygen began to increase. Earth becomes a humid swamp full of the scuttlings of giant insects. The new skeleton developed by plants is lignin and nothing lives on the earth than can eat it. Trees fall in the forest and the carbon they have taken from the air lies immutable on the earth. What today we call fossil fuels are created in this period of run-away climate change. Finally the mycelium of fungus figures out how to eat dead plant matter. With this new accord mushrooms and plants enter a cyclic dance of recycling, along with added flourishes of hormonal communication, and complex mutual interdependence, while phosphates and sugars are silently and invisibly traded between these vast interpenetrating bodies of non-animal flesh. Woods may look calm to an observer using vertebrate eyes, but they hide a lot of frenetic activity below the surface.

The density of species interactions accelerates away in a tangled union of forms. The worms have worms within them. Co-operation flourishes and mutual aid exists. One small fish cleans the gills of another; tolerated by the snapping jaws of sharks, it rasps away bacteria from its mighty host. All these webs are woven together, tighter and tighter. Mycelium of fungus eats into dead plant matter, liberating nourishment for living plants that in turn pull down atmospherically derived molecules that feed their mushrooms. Insects become so closely related to plants that chemically speaking it's hard to know where one entity ends and the other begins. Complex food webs become the Gordian knots of Gaia.

Meanwhile the beasts are coming. Vast animals, gigantic lizards are abroad on a global scale: 'Here be dragons!' The dance of predator and prey is elaborated into a million arabesques of bony forehead, plated backs, spiked thumbs and terrible teeth. Larger animals ramp up their stamina, there's plenty to be done; nest building, fighting, grazing, scavenging, mating, and a thousand more complex behaviours that the fossil record barely hints at. The stage is set for new forms of lung, tissues that permit greater stamina, heating the blood and turning sunbathing lizards into fired-up hot-blooded types. Between the tree-trunk legs of vast sauropods skitter chattering hairy shrews.

And hand-in-hand with this carnival of creation goes the stink of death. Life builds death into itself in order to maintain its stability. The caspase enzyme cascade sits shadowy and ubiquitous in our cells. Death is the essential for complex multi-cellular life, limiting, recycling, and forming a firewall against those viral phages and DNA transcription errors that would overrun an immortal organism. Death is essential for the functioning of the whole network of life. In the bloated corpses of vertebrates millions of tiny bacterial lives emerge, to say nothing of the corpse pecking avians that straddle the carcass, munching on protein rich eyeballs.

Death builds itself into the spawning of salmon and octopus. It embeds itself in the mating rituals of the mantis. Animals like us that cleverly seek to extend their life spans meet it rising up in cancerous growths of DNA run amok.

Visited from outside the planet death comes on swift wings in the form of meteor strikes and violent climate changes. But the ever-proliferating variation in forms of cells continues, the safety net is the near invulnerable web of bacteria beneath the more complex and showy forms of life. So what if a comet wipes out huge numbers of creatures and changes the ecology from tropical heat to bone shattering cold? Life will rise again, spew out new forms into each niche. Sometimes these manifestations will be wildly different to those that have gone before but more frequently they will seem oddly familiar. The world of the biosphere, adapting to the geosphere, throws out the ichthyosaurus and the dolphin, the pterosaur and the bat.

Complex minds that imagine the world grew in the ancient oceans. But now these minds emerge, in part, from the energy hungry wad of electrified fat that crowns the naked body of an ape. Like ants, these creatures have found great power in creating a collective form of intelligence, a society that can achieve far more than lone individuals. Barking and singing and chattering, these apes are perfecting a form of symbolic communication, an aural version of the cuttlefish's colourful language. Battering shellfish with rocks to retrieve their nourishing contents, these animals use anvils like sea otters. In imitation of the weaverbird these creatures decorate their nests with brightly coloured ochre and iridescent feathers. Monkey see, monkey do.

These collections of cells. These wondrous cascades of chemical complexity. They appear to themselves as singular beings because of their necessarily limited perception of time and space. But like all life they are in reality a flow, a process, a colony, and a conspiracy of microbes. They vastly extend the world of created objects. Technology arises, flints that cut, obsidian blades that scrape, bamboo spears. The traces of material culture are driven into a wider variety of forms by the rapidly emerging noosphere, realm of ideation. A felt sense of mathematical space gives rise to the realisation of intricate weaving and sewing. A generic understanding of chemistry allows fruits to be processed so that the indigestible becomes edible and good. Identity and difference create clan symbols and an imagined sense of the world is painted onto the roofs of caves. The life force writes itself onto the fabric of the geosphere as representation, as imagination and as meaning. Language, like DNA with its finite number of basic rules, creates an infinite number of possible utterances.

These animals begin to know that they die. They bury their dead. They are devastating hunters. They learn to carry water and their young on their migrations. They begin to have a sense of time and carve their intuition as lunation coded shapes on bones. They see faces in rocks and tree branches, and they feel love and dread for places as well as each other, giving names to genii locorum. They attain a new chemical power, that of combustion, and learn to capture and make fire. This gives them heat and light to illuminate their explorations of the underworld. They make their way into caves.

In these subterranean places some of the first experiments in intentional trance begin. The cellular patterns of trillions of biological reactions conspire to formulate the means of gnosis: rhythmic music, fasting, magical plants, dancing. Considered from its individual perspective these animals imagine they know how to contact the life force of the universe. The deep base throb of the drum begins, and in that darkness of the deep, sparkling entoptic images burst into sight. An infinite gallery of ideas, glimmering like stars in the night of the prehistoric human mind. The Stars are but thistles in that waste, pregnant seed heads that burst, releasing their strange cargo into vast space.

Evolution

The description of evolution given here has been vastly simplified, and we must admit to it covering only a few of the developments Life on Earth has undergone since the crust first cooled. Our aim however is not to be a textbook; we wanted to demonstrate the enormous time frame life has existed for, and how the gradual increasing complexity organisms have adopted (in order to slow the slide towards entropy) has given rise to amazing diversity; while evolutionary history tends to focus necessarily on physical fossils and therefore the organisms as individuals, the more far reaching implications of these physical remains must take priority when trying to form a more coherent picture of life. Behaviours of these organisms, and the way these affect the environment around them, including the biosphere, geosphere and the atmosphere, are at least as important as the description of the physical bodies they possess. An account of a human as a bag containing the various chemical constituents does not describe a human at all. Without awareness and appreciation of all the behavioural and environmental modifying results of humans, a purely biological description leaves us none the wiser.

So from this perspective then, the evolutionary history of the Earth can be seen as an exponential climb towards increased levels of complexity of behaviour, as well as physical and social complexity.

From internal monitoring and regulation (homeostasis), to reproduction through division (thus overcoming limits of growth), creation of complex molecules from simple ones (chemotrophism), developing a sense of external awareness, movement through the external environment, consumption of other lifeforms (chemoorganoheterotrophism), death, sex, emotions, and the ability to create internal models of external worlds not directly sensed, we (the living cosmos) have expanded our identities beyond the single point living cell to far beyond the stars we view each night. Our boundaries of perceived Self may theoretically stop at the skin, but in actuality extends to the tools we use, the clothes we wear, the food we eat, the land we inhabit, the people we identify with.

For our species, identification with other life forms comes as second nature. Mimicking behaviour and survival strategies of divers creatures, human animals have sidestepped the long evolutionary haul to borrow from the tried and tested ways they observe around them, can even exchange such ways across vast swathes of space and time. By acknowledging the connections between different lives, we show our thanks for the hardships endured by those ancestors who discovered this practice, and re-awaken our current status quo to learn more from the well tried and tested techniques of all the kingdoms at hand.

The results of selection pressures over millions of years on living information systems demonstrate to us how complex abstract informational systems might flourish sustainably; the worlds of finance and economics, social behaviour of large groups, have begun to appreciate the strategies that population biology has revealed. Ecology holds much in the way of enlightening our views on the laws of supply and demand, providing visions of divers long-term symbiotic interspecies relationship networks that allow all involved to flourish.

The several monotheistic religions of the most recent millennia have done us a huge disservice by popularising the worldview of a single group as special and separate from all others (e.g., Christian vs Pagan concepts of religion, a dichotomy which can now be seen as patently absurd considering the unquestionable origins of Christianity as merely one cult of many in the group now referred to as pagan). This spiritual distinction has been mapped onto other major fundamental distinctions between humans and other life forms. With its origins on a basic biological drive to distinguish Self from Other, then Family group from Other, it is hardly surprising that this illusory distinction between Manmade and Natural worlds still prevails today.

But this emphasis of unique qualities prevents us from recognising the common links we have with so much of Life. Man is a special animal, however this illusion of a quantum leap of difference in our uniqueness existed because the many other closely related species of which we are one branch have all vanished, for climatic and other reasons. Our continued existence as the species which has mastered metaphor and meaning lies on a scale which ought to contain other sibling species with lesser and maybe even greater abilities in this matter; to lose sight of this is to condemn ourselves to a life of blinkered solitude. We have built walls to keep out the monsters of the wild, but these walls block out so much more. By opening a few doors, perhaps we can extend our perceptions beyond this prisoner mentality, and walk out of the institutional lifestyle which surrounds us. For we play a part in the world, a role that the world itself produced. We are the fruit of larger forces interacting. We need to step up, and play our role well, as translators and communicators, as visionaries for all the forms that life takes on our planet, as it continues to evolve.

This book makes a ladder to prop against the walls of our isolation, to look above the parapet, to see how we might discover ways to climb out of our restrictive self imposed exile from Nature.

Have fun, and learn things.

Elucidation

This book decided to emerge as a collage. Instead of a simple coherent history or linear narrative, we formed a many coloured patchwork of words, experiences and ideas. Our two bodies and their third mind gave rise to a multitude of perspectives, a chorus of voices. The conversation of these voices is centred around one specific name for that ground of lived existence, what some native cultures have called The Great Spirit. Such a name is of course a human artefact, an anthropomorphisation which expresses the notion that all life, indeed all existence, is a thing; woven from threads of material, matter's warp and weft. This fabric could be described by generalised names like 'God' or 'Goddess', or some more specific conception of deity. We could have woven this story around the notion of an impersonal universal energy; chi or prana or life force. We might have chosen terms from the language of science, such as evolution, that marvellous mutability of form and action expressed through the universe as a whole and here on earth in what we conceptualise as those special organic systems, our own tribe.

But our wyrd has been to choose something else, a less well known name which reveals new patterns normally hidden deep within the weave of the perennial wisdom.

So this is the story of that name, representing for the authors the arising of the self-aware universe, anchored to an obscure arrangement of eight letters.

We present to you, dear reader, this palimpsest of many years' work, overwritten by our two hands until we cannot tell ourselves who wrote which part for the other. What you make of our offering, we cannot predict. We wish you luck in finding your own valuables as you mine through our ore.

First Contact

Something is pressing to come in, something big. That something appears beneath our history, shuddering, a great figure concealed under the fabric of reality. As it wakes, its motions send shockwaves across space-time. This thing is emerging, and human consciousness awakens to it, through it. We can see it lurking if we stride back through time, catch glimpses of its form and meaning. Some imagine it as a glittering object at the end of history. Some fear it as the incursion of abominable alien gods from the spaces between the stars. We welcome it, this force, this feeling, this enticingly ever-unveiling mystery.

Our name for this mystery is Baphomet.

Baphomet is a glyph, a word, a signal for something much larger. This glyph first appears with the persecution of The Order of the Knights Templar. It peers out at us, more than half a millennium later, horned and devilish from 19th century French occultism. It appears again within The Order of the Eastern Templars or OTO. More recently this name inflamed the minds of the founders of the Magical Pact of the Illuminates of Thanateros or IOT. Now it has broken through, beyond the precincts of any one temple. This book, in part, traces the gradual emergence of this new deity. Other voices in this volume weave further strands of this entity's rich tapestry, the tracery revealing this Spirit within the commonplace. They describe the evolution of life on our planet and the memes that swarm around the curious relationship between those counterpoints our culture has created; Humanity and Nature. It is this interwoven relationship of all that lives which we know as Baphomet.

From the beginning of life on this planet this thing was always coming. Encoded within the spiralling snake, coiled in the heart of every cell. This entity, this feeling, is what we call Baphomet.

Goddess of all life on the face of the Earth, above, beside and below the human world we inhabit, we beseech you to show your form to us, reveal your ways to us that we may learn! In the cloud filled skies above, the plant filled world we walk, the cavernous underworld below, your signs *appear to us, if we would but heed them. We need your* deepest wisdom, O Baphomet. We tillers of the soil, who believe we rule the earth, we have power but we now need to learn how to practise our new craft healthily, because even after only 9,000 years, we've clearly messed up in a fundamental way. Yet for millions of years of Life, You kept the soil growing and thriving; tell us your secrets, O great fertility god! Tell us your occult knowledge, that we may eat of the land and yet not destroy it! How do you take on so many divers forms yet remain as an ineffable functioning communicating whole? Baphomet, we call upon you, manifest to us, teach us the long game! Show us how to maintain integrity as both individuals and community! You who are Lord of this world, burning deep in the geosphere – arise!

Well that's humans for you. Always grubbing around in the dirt. That's what we do, our species, we dig. The most ingenious form of worm, burrowing and bringing material from the A horizon upwards to the surface. More than this, humans dig down to the deepest caves, drill shafts into the earth. We seek all manner of treasures there, avaricious gnomes that we are; oil, precious stones, uranium, gold – the raw materials of our technological prowess. Metal, so important that it gets its own elemental status in Chinese esotericism. Clay, the basis of most creation myths, the prima mater. To cultivate the food to fill our bellies we've been playing with dirt for at least 10,000 years. Slyly slipping seeds in the womb of the earth, harvesting grains, fruits and tubers. Deeper than this, with redoubtable metal, we turn the earth, as though mixing a giant cauldron. We till the soil, speeding up its metabolic rate, chuck in some selectively bred DNA and *voilà!* A few back-breaking months later we can have cakes and ale.

Part of the trouble (if it is a trouble and not some elaborate Gaian-supermind intention) is that as we plough and mine we cast up immense volumes of carbon dioxide into the sky. With our fires, kindled so innocently in the cave mouth, we add to this process. Flames from coal and oil, the marrowbones and blood of the planet, accelerate our technologically achieved exo-metabolism of ancient carbon into heat, light and cooking. We've lit our hearths with the roots of many mountains and changed the heavens in so doing.

Like a prayer to the gods of climate change we offer up this invisible suffumigation CO_2, plus a subtle concoction of other gases. Lately some of our offerings have been so elaborate – elegant and novel molecules – that the gods of chaos have smiled and bestowed on us their blessings in great abundance.

Where once we could plough the earth and plant our crops, now desert sweeps across the land. Where once ice stood miles thick now glaciers weep into the rising sea. Where once the broad patterns of weather were predictable now the carbon-based butterfly flaps its wings and the seasonal rhythm breaks down into discord. Mountains cut down to reach the treasures within, acres of land removed to find the black gold, millions of tons of water formed into artificial lakes collectively heavy enough to alter the spin of our planet.

(Hail Eris!)

This is the Thanatos side of the Baphomet goat. Manifest in one form as the horned and hoofed eating engine that plodded inexorably across the Fertile Crescent. Then there was the felling of the ancient palm forests of the Tigris-Euphrates valley. The throwing up of our cities that march their way across yet more of the land, spilling out new suburbs, bigger and bigger, age after age. Emblematic of the whole process, the horns of our goats rip the bark from the trees, the teeth eat and eat and eat.

Not to blame the poor sabbat goat or Passover lamb for everything. It is our species; us ape men, which are really the überconsumers. We arrive on an island and, rejoicing, discover that there is a large flightless bird that resides there. Their numbers are prodigious, and they are shite at running. We pick them up as easily as fat fruits and take them back to camp. We cook them over the driftwood fire, they taste finger lickin' good!

Eventually some of us realise that these tasty fowl are getting trickier to find. Finally someone bags the last brace and that's that. Luckily for us there's plenty of fruit on the island. We could even try tilling the soil and get some grain growing. And there are, of course, plenty more fish in the sea, as the saying goes. (Or at least there used to be.)

In the tarot the card The Tower is ascribed the Hebrew letter Pe – the mouth. Humans are a mouth, we eat up everything we can and, richly nourished, throw the spires of our culture ever higher. Hell, we've even transported our bodies to the moon and back! We've travelled by proxy, on robotic ships that sail on sunshine, as far as the outer reaches of our solar system, and taken tourist photographs. Engraved upon these vessels we have sent postcards to the inhabitants of Deep Space.

But this century the walls of Jericho, of Babel, of debt-based Capitalism, come tumbling down. We're woken by the bolt from the blue, the consciousness of how much disruption we've wrought upon the earth's support systems, of our position as expendable - one of many life forms that inhabit this planet. Poised on this cliff do we step off like the Fool? What comes after The Tower? Ah yes, The Star.

Hope, the One Star in Sight. Nothing if not adaptable we humans. Our global awareness, gained perhaps just in time, before the meltdown, might do it. That awareness which peers out of the cave of Self and apprehends the Big Picture.

There is no alternative to this awakening except extinction. Appreciating the game of ecological consequences is not about a dismal realisation that we're all going to die. It goes beyond that into a sweeping, opening realm of possibility. We emerge from the cave into the light of knowledge. That knowledge is awful, awesome, and sublime: the gnosis of the World.

We emerge from the trance and hear the million voices singing the song of life.

If we can act on this knowledge, and not be overwhelmed or ignorant of it, we may just have a chance of reaching the stars. To continue our exploration of inner and outer space together forever.

When we consider interstellar space, we might envisage many kinds of distant alien intelligences. But the only intelligence we know exists for sure is our own. Perhaps we're the first, destined to carry the wave of sentience out into the universe? We may be the origin, the panspermia for the rest of the galaxy. Certainly we are potentially part of the gametes of Gaia, her egg and sperm. The reproductive structures of a planet may look like us; a clever monkey who can dig and knows that it's going to die.

Can we see ourselves as a whole, blend our self-sentience with this global perspective? From that hole of the earth, climb higher inside our magick, raise ourselves, eyes curiously dilated, into the overground world. What could we wise apes achieve? Perhaps in a million years some being with human inheritance will read these words on a far distant world. Out of the cave of our home world we will have come. From a global vision, born on the wave of better resource use, that leads us into outer space.

Whether it is us, our particular configuration of consciousness that proliferates Gaia's seed into space does not matter (except as a point of personal pride). But it could be us; would we be up to the job?

Our species has stolen the fire from heaven and, like Lucifer, pride isn't something we're short of.

As the Old Man of the Mountains said: we are here to go.

Out of the Eastern Temple

And what of origins? What does history, that million-voiced record of myth, tell us? Where does this name begin - 'Baphomet'? The year is 1307 and The Poor Fellow-Soldiers of Christ and of the Temple of Solomon, better known as The Knights Templar, are about to get busted. An avalanche of accusations is made against the members of this powerful military Order who have been in the business of protecting Christian pilgrims in the Holy Land since 1129. Among these accusations, brought against them by King Philip IV 'the Fair' of France, is that the Templars are idolaters. Their idol is a head, a cat, a many-faced form, a skull stuffed with grain... Whatever the details might be, its name, though confessed by only a few, is Baphomet.

When the cops raided them the Templars were already on their downward spiral. By 1291 they had lost control of almost all of their Christian outposts in the Middle East. Though both powerful and pervasive as a power block in Mediaeval Europe, a combination of suspicious secrecy and political misjudgement would bring them low. The fat Templar treasury was another reason for their trial. Folk said as much at the time. But we shouldn't dismiss their impeachment as being a one-dimensional story of Crown avarice visited on the knights' coffers. There is, perhaps, something more at work here.

The Templar trial provided the pattern upon which much of the post Medieval witch-hunt was based. The allegations of orgiastic behaviour, sodomy, denial of Christ and idolatry became the stock in trade of the next few centuries of torture and terror. Modern history, and indeed recent Vatican documents, assure us that the Templars were not guilty. They were framed, persecuted.

But let's look a little more closely at this curious case. One particular charge, which some historians have thrown away as a 'mere technicality', is perhaps pertinent to our Work – namely that the Templars took each other's confession. Their crime; not using a *bona fide* Ordained Priest to do so. Seems that the Brothers were doing it for themselves.

And what of this abominable idol? Baphomet - the word occurs earlier than the Templar Trials. Most famously in the melancholic writing of a troubadour from 1265, possibly a Templar himself.

> "Then it is really foolish to fight the Turks, now that Jesus Christ no longer opposes them. They have vanquished the Franks and Tartars and Armenians and Persians, and they continue to do so. And daily they impose new defeats on us; for God, who used to watch on our behalf is now asleep, and Bafometz puts forth his power in support of the Sultan."

Any historian worth their discourse will explain that Baphomet (whichever of the variegated spellings we prefer) is simply the Infidel's rendering of Muhammed. The irony that Islam, with its proscription against representation in religious art, should be the imagined origin of such idolatry raises a wry grin.

As our troubadour Brother writes about God falling asleep, Europe begins to be infected by the Christ of Sorrow. Throughout the later medieval period images of Jesus are increasingly focused on the torture of Our Lord. More and more thorns tear the flesh of icons (note – that's icons, objects leading the thoughts of the viewer towards the Holy, as distinct from idols which are themselves the objects of worship) in the Churches. As the Holy Land slips from the grasp of Christendom, and the Black Death rampages through the continent, many people can hear the band tuning up for the symphony of Apocalypse. So Baphomet strides into this time, onto the stage where many believe the final curtain call is not far off. Baphomet emerges in a time of terror and of loss. Baphomet is born out of the secrecy of the Templars, and in such secret spaces all manner of dangerous ideas may ferment.

A solidly sober Templar historian writes:

> "The essentials of magical practice are concealment, plotting and secrecy. A magical accusation almost always includes the charge, or at least the implication, of conspiracy."

Concealed in the name Baphomet there is much more than a wilful misinterpretation of The Prophet of Islam (Peace Be Upon Him). This word was to be the tiny eight-letter mote around which a mythic pearl of great price would grow.

Baphomet withdraws after the Templar roasting is done. Disappears off the diabolical Who's Who of post-medieval Grimoires. We don't seem to get another name check until the Masonic agitator Johann August Starck (1741-1816) picks Baphomet as the proposed deity for his ceremony 'Canon of the Temple', a rather stylish rite which perhaps deserves the adjective 'Satanic'.

Before Starck though, the story of the Templars, the myth of their rise, fall and occult knowledge, had filtered into the esoteric tradition. Plenty of people had their opinions about the trial. Dante protested their innocence, the alchemist Arnau of Vilanova thought they were bang to rights. But it is in 1531, when Henry Cornelius Agrippa published his magnum opus of Renaissance magic De Occulta Philosophia, that the story of Baphomet begins its re-emergence.

Agrippa distinguishes his brand of occultism from malefic sorcery, "…the scandalous and impious practices of black magic…" While Agrippa is writing, the Hammer of the Witches has been falling steadily for two centuries. By acknowledging the guilt of the Knights Templar Agrippa certainly isn't bucking any trends (Vatican opinion of the time was still that the Templars had it coming). But what he is doing is identifying Templar heresy as the pursuit of black magic. And if that is the case then Baphomet is at the dark heart of their occult wickedness. Clearly, as Starck later surmised, Baphomet is identical with Satan.

During the Renaissance plenty of writers were convinced that there really was something fishy going on within the Templar Brotherhood. Some claimed that Templar novices were brought into a cave for their initiation. There they would spit upon the cross and fall down and worship an image covered with human skin sporting two glowing eyes. Women would be admitted to the ritual and unspeakable orgies would, naturally, take place.

Hang on! Let's return to ground zero. Could the Templars, having hung around in the Middle East for so long, really have become contaminated with some heretical doctrine?

The Order of Poor Knights of the Temple of Solomon was founded some two decades after the First Crusade captured Jerusalem in 1099. King Baldwin III of Jerusalem welcomed these religious warriors and offered them quarters in his palace which, it was said, stood on the site of the Temple of King Solomon. To the west of this first Templar territory, on an artificial enhanced trapezoid of rock (the Haram-al-Sharif platform) stands the Dome of the Rock. This eight-sided structure is one of the holiest sites of Islam (it's here that Mohammed, strapped to the booster rocket of the angel Gabriel, jets off to heaven). The Dome, or rather the sacred rock beneath it, is the Jewish Holy of Holies. Here, in the darkened tabernacle, resided the Arc of the Covenant. Here the Third Temple would be raised and, according to Orthodox Judaism, it's then that the Messiah will show up. Given this fact it is hardly surprising that today the Knesset is regularly petitioned to start both building the Third Temple and slaughtering horned animals on the site.

Back down the road, at the Temple of Solomon, there is certainly magic in the air. The very stones of the first temple were moved by demons under Solomon's command. On the edge of history, where polytheism gives way to monotheist belief, Solomon makes his conjurations. His temple stood until Nebuchadnezzar II took his turn at that popular pastime of enslaving the Jews. He torched the place. Weeping, God's chosen people were led into bondage. Through the Neo-Babylonian king's magnificent Ishtar gate of blue and gold, emblazoned with lions, dragons and daisies, they went down into Babylon and slavery.

Unsurprisingly the Temple of Solomon had all the usual kit. A complex design drenched in symbolism; the twin pillars of Boaz and Jachin, chambers rammed with treasure, even an indoor pool.

> "And he made a molten sea, ten cubits from the one brim to the other: it was round all about, and his height was five cubits: and a line of thirty cubits did compass it round about." 1 Kings 7:23

Perhaps this pool is a nod to the Ancient Egyptian and Babylonian practice of maintaining a representation of the apsu, the deep, the primordial ocean, in the heart of the sacred space.

Solomon, like his Templar houseguests of two millennia later, was also accused of idolatry.

THE BOOK OF BAPHOMET 45

*Fig 1   Astaroth, prince of Hell, from J.A.S. Collin de Plancy,
Dictionnaire Infernal. Original illustration by Louis Breton,
engraved by M. Jarrault.*

The theme of idolatry is an important one! Worshipping the visible, tangible world rather than an abstracted God vouchsafed to us through the interpretative powers of the priesthood.

Like the Templars, Solomon is seduced by the lure of strange gods. He falls for foreign women, probably gets it on with the Queen of Sheba and turns from Jehovah to the Goddess Ashtoreth. Goddess of the eight pointed star emblem signifying the planet Venus.

Ashtoreth, Astarte and Apophrodite; Goddess of fucking and war. In Jewish myth she is a demon of lust. The medieval sorcerer, armed with Solomon's Key as his grimoire, would meet her as, "...the impure Venus of the Syrians, whom they represent with the head of an ass or of a bull, and the breasts of a woman." (Spot those horns and Setian ears.) By 1863 ceremonial magicians had a photofit of this entity. Jacques Collin de Plancy handily provides this in his *Dictionnaire Infernal*.

A salacious woman with a snake. We'll see more of her later...

What else do we know about King Solomon? Well he possessed a flying carpet, probably stained scarlet with the local dye plant for soft furnishings, Syrian rue. With the high percentage of psychedelic harmaline alkaloids in this plant a magical flight could be guaranteed. When not airborne Solomon sat upon a throne around which were crowded animals wrought in gold: a lion, an ox, a wolf, a tiger, a camel and a peacock, cat and eagle. Totem beasts crouching at his feet, this King of the Jews looks more like the Lord of Animals than the earthly face of that 'dry desert god with no sense of humour'. But the Templars, those founding fathers of the Baphomet myth, were they as guilty of the same creeping paganism as Solomon?

There are hints of syncretism (or heresy), some encoded in Templar architecture which serves to keep a whole industry of psychic questing alive and well in the modern period. One example; England, St Michael's Church in Garway, Herefordshire. From the M5 motorway leave at junction 8 and move on to the M50, up to Ross-on-Wye. At the end of the M50, travel a short distance on the A40 to Bridstow and then turn on to the A49. Four miles down this road turn onto the B4521, eight miles later make a small right turn; stop and look around. This Church was founded in 1180 and there are Templar carvings on the outside of the building. A host of curious glyphs and foliate heads, serpents curling around a staff. But these are all perfectly intelligible bits and bobs of ecclesiastical masonry. More interesting are the Norman arches with zigzag designs, undoubtedly cribbed from Middle Eastern architecture. The Moorish influence is certainly in evidence here. Then there is the swastika on the outside wall. The whirling thunderbolt of Indian mysticism rubs shoulders with more conventional Christian imagery. These sites remind us emphatically of the Middle Eastern roots of monotheism and the polytheistic ferment from which it in turn emerges. The Templars, as crusader knights, were re-connecting their European Christianity to its eastern roots.

Later Templar myths links the Order to the assassins, those hashish steeped dissidents the Isma'ilis. Leader of their Order, the Old Man of the Mountains Hassan-i Sabbah reputedly said on his deathbed "Nothing is True, Everything is Permitted". Proof for some of the ancient roots of the Illuminati conspiracy. Curious then that Hassan, our supposedly wild-eyed radical, is also said to have had his son executed for drunkenness. However allegations of this connection are much older than Idries Shah or Robert Anton Wilson. William of Tyre, writing before the Templars were cast down, accuses them of receiving tribute of 2000 gold pieces from the Isma'ilis. The Templars are, says William, guilty of greed and arrogance, their thirst for treasure far outstripping their devotion to God and Holy Mother Church.

Fire Underground

I work, rubbing sticks together in the cave. Sweating with the effort, intense physical effort and concentration on the repetitive task, emotions held at bay while my attention focuses on the point of contact, the junction between the two bodies of wood. Friction, that's what I'm after, movement and juxtaposition in one, the tinder carefully prepared lies waiting for the spark. Just a few more minutes…

The day filled with sunshine waits outside. So why do I squat here in the dark? I can't see my hand in front of my face even. My mind's eye holds the memories of touch sensations though. I know the location of everything I need. So many times I have ignited the fire, my body knows the way as surely as it knows how to breathe, I can see the objects as if it were noon. Familiarity.

You can see me too, without light yet, a figure hunched over in total blackness, head bowed over my work, you can see the wood and the pile of dried fungus, moss and twigs, the stack of kindling and the few logs for later on to provide a steady base for the fire once lit. You can see the rocky walls of the cave arching high overhead, the hard floor. Grey. So think how much more I can see here where I have been so many times; I may not have visual cues from Now but I have the advantage over you, I have seen this place and these things before. I know my fire making equipment, every knot and twist, every curve. I know the eight-rayed star design carved into the objects that mark them as mine.

I gathered the fuel for my fire in the sunlight, hot on my back, carrying the solidified air and stored light into the darkness, wanting to see in the realm of the dead. Here nothing grows. No divine nurturing happens in this space below the surface. No light, no green plants, no herbivores, no predators. No people.

Except me

The sound of my breathing fills the space, echoing off the walls. I can hear water dripping in distant tunnels. Aha! At last I see a few glows. I keep the wood turning, nearly there, like the pre-orgasm moment when you have to keep moving even though you desperately want to give in to the wave of pleasure, keep going that bit longer and then, yes! I pick up the embers; tip them oh so carefully into the bundle of tinder and blow.

Having lit the fire the world around me does something strange and beautiful; it becomes visible to my wide-open pupils, gaining definition, size, colours, dimensions, while simultaneously shrinking from the limitless possibilities it had before. As I glance up, I can see the walls instead of imagining them. Back to work, I must keep watching the young fire, feeding it morsels of delicate twigs until it grows strong enough to live alone for minutes at a time. Glimpses of the walls and the figures begin to reappear in my memory from previous times here. Stars, spirals. Points of light and colour. Shapes on the rocks that look a bit like animals, if I just dotted the eye here, and added a pair of horns there…

The fire crackles. I use dry wood that burns bright and fast, this fire is not for endurance but intensity, light not heat. I shall be here only a matter of hours, here deep inside.

So what am I doing here? I have travelled away from the world to a place inside it. Retreat to; or from? Well both of course. From, all that I know to be real and meaningful, all my established patterns of behaviour, my fellow travellers, human and otherwise, away from the weather, the trees, the soil, the substances of the universe I experience everyday. I step away from them. They can survive without me for a few hours. I have walked into the place of Otherness. Because I am a magician, 'One who Can'. Because I am a shaman, needing to contact the spirits larger than the individuals of my tribe, my family. I want to tell them how we're doing, ask questions of them, and let them ask me questions. Think of it like reporting back to base from an expedition. A phone call to your mum on Sunday afternoon, to let her know what's up in your life. A diary entry where you can pour out all your worries, to find most of them dissolve like mist when exposed to the critical burning gaze of a wider viewpoint.

After these meetings I can never decide whether I have called to the spirits or they to me, which of us invokes the presence of the other, and these days I don't much care. Cause and effect, the linear narrative that trapped me from day 1 of a for apple, b for ball, c for cat, no longer holds me in its thrall. Free to dip into one stream or another like the poets do, writing itself takes on the life of a multidimensional tapestry, a web of meanings emerging on multiple readings many of which I shall never comprehend myself, taking on a life of its own as eyes that are not I scan the page left to right (or if translated by then, right to left, up and down, however the language works…)

My Myers-Briggs personality type ENFP means that I swim in a consciousness surrounded on all sides by sensory input. I take in all the perceptions, I feel them, and I live from them. This makes me very good at empathising with people and the world in general. It means I have almost no sense of a self apart from the world around me. What happens to this persona in conditions of sensory deprivation? The slightest trigger, the smallest seed of an idea, explodes to create whole universes of double entendre, symbolisms, metaphors of word/image/meaning. Here in the cave away from everything I have carried myself, and a bag.

Inside the bag, like any good shaman's bag, are objects that make up the universe. I packed my bag this morning and in it I put…

A gleaming mother of pearl covered shell, millions of years old, an ammonite (Named for the horned god Ammon, whose temples in the Egyptian desert attracted the feet of so many rulers, the mythical ancestor of Alexander the Great, who was often depicted with his curly horns; disliked by the Zoroastrians, and considered as ally of the enemy of their hero god Ahuramazda, Alexander's publicity pictures on his coins may well provide the origin of the iconography of the familiar horned devil vs good god); a shell which grew in a tropical ocean, far away in space and time. Life from before.

My bear talisman. Carved from a clear piece of rock crystal, bought from a market stall minutes after the visionquest that revealed the bear spirit to me, it followed me home and runs around me like some people have a dog. It smells the world and leads me to places of power, things that are good to eat. It reassures me with its shaggy presence. The talisman that gives me a bodily link to my spirit animal lives in a black pouch with green and gold threads to draw it closed.

My wand. Today I use my holly wand; a slender piece of straight wood stripped of bark and shaped at one end to form a slanting point. Runes are risted into its surface. The length is one cubit, the length of my forearm and hand combined. Traditional Egyptian wand length.

A silvery bowl. Beaten from pure steel, the hammer marks still visible as part of the decoration, I love the timelessness of this chalice. It will never rust, never lose its shine. I carry it in a dark green pouch.

A small bottle filled with sacrament. Vodka, mushrooms, a tab of acid. Herbs from sacred places. Stones from sacred times I attended. A rune stave I made, burnt, and collected the ashes from.

Tobako and papers. This plant ally and I have a strong link, it helps me regain my mundane self, walking that line between worlds, as shamans must, never losing awareness of the reason I travel outside the world in order to look inside it. Which is also why I wear on my wrist a leather band studded with squares of metal, given to me down the pub by a mate.

A larger bottle, of water. For drinking. And anointing myself.

Food. Fruits, dried and fresh, some bread I made yesterday. For protein I have brought seeds and a few nuts.

The fossilised shell has been consecrated on previous occasions to Baphomet, the godform I intend to contact here now.

And I have in my bag some paint to use to decorate whatever I need to. My body, or the cave, or the things I have carried with me.

A blanket to sit on, wrap myself in, as necessary.

Not in my bag but on my back in a black bag of its own, I have carried in my drum, a single skin stretched over a green wooden form. The beater is made of yew wood. Until the fire burns brighter this must stay in its silent state, the skin will be too damp here to sing until I have the means to dry it taut.

My plan is to chant, to listen, to dance, keep the fire fed, until the Other world here takes over as normality. When that happens, when I am a figure that is in the cave and that's all there is, then I shall state my intent "It is my will to invoke Baphomet!" and I shall drink a mouthful of the sacrament. I shall confess all the problems my tribe has right now, how the failings of circumstance and personalities have given us issues. (Some of these will have been dealt with already, others outstanding situations in need of resolution.) My tribe I count on different levels, my family, my friends, my magickal brothers and sisters, the island I live on, the planetary wide community of people, the ecological world of the alive and the once alive. Only then can I perform the invocation as so many times before. Accessing that one moment of wider consciousness that never stays the same, yet always resonates with the eternal song.

Everything in a state of constant change.

As Baphomet, I know what to do when there is a solution. I code this into the movements of my horse, the songs and rhythms of her drumbeat, to carry the answer back to the world of distractions all packaged up into images, words and other communicable forms. I give the wider perspective, the long term view, without taking away from the limits of the tiny; I know what it is to live as an inch high plant in the sand dunes as well as the crust of the earth lasting for aeons. Seeing from all angles, that is the power I can bestow. In the Chaos of the Normal I shake and tilt the crystal of a brain until a pattern appears, Apophenian inspiration emerging, as I move the universes into alignment, so the picture leaps out, and the key to the puzzle drops into the hand of the magician. Turn!

But, for now I have not yet reached this point in time. I sit by the growing fire, warmth emanating now, and I look at the pictures on the walls. Firelight moves, gives the lines movement as shadows dance. Animals and other figures look back at me. Some I saw myself on previous visits, and set free from the rockface; some are far older, marking a gap in contact with the world we live in of thousands of years. Quite how this happened I cannot say, somewhere we lost the practices of reaching this far down, in, out. On this continent, anyway.

Too much star gazing, perhaps? Looking up to light filled space for knowledge, instead of at our own world? Seeking for answers from above, navigating to find new territories to master, seeing what crops we could grow in these new realms. But in the excitement we forgot about our health, our quality of life, fixated on numbers that go up, storing up things worthless to our lives, as well as the worthy. A linear obsession with simplistic calculations…the Measurable Universe Delusion, started by recording the counts of tributes, populations, and starry wisdom.

This moment in history, every moment, we decide what kind of world we wish to make, to live in. As we now see the first signs of the collapse of our apparent steady state culture which has emerged over the last few thousand years, we have the sensory enhancing technologies to show what happens if we continue in a business as usual scenario. We have really no choice, the only way to go shouts out, plain as the nose on your face. You know. I point at you.

This fire underground that I light shines brighter in my vision now than the sun. As I enter the entheogenic state the inner light amplifies all, objects glow with luminous importance in their own right. I listen and watch to see which things need moving, which links need to be made or broken, twisting here, tweaking there, cutting and splicing the threads of connection that are my web. I weave an entire fabric from what has gone before, from what I/we want to come after. This eye of the needle we pass through, this Now, is the only moment we can do this. Reworked the fabric can look shoddy if not regularly unpicked and tidied. Still, like the axe of my grandfather it stays the same however often the components get replaced.

One day I will be replaced, not with the same body, but my role in the world, if a space exists for it to be filled, will shape for itself another shaman, another magician, another priest for the tribe. Another voice to shout so the gods can hear, to whisper the soft words of love from those greater than the individual can comprehend, another set of limbs to walk and embrace and create. Another eye to see, in the light of the sun.

Caves. Why so much imagery about caves? The dark and the light, the dead and the living, the realms of the psychonaut and the world of the ordinary.

Houses, the structures we have in our cities and urban areas since the dawn of civilization, have more closely resembled caves than the natural, living world. There are no plants here, and until the invention of sheet glass using the float method, no natural light to speak of. No wild animals wander through the rooms, no wind stirs your hair, nor rain falls on your face.

Why am I so obsessing with caves when I'm writing about Baphomet? Caves are Mithraic, surely. Mithras, god of the Roman soldier, the same deity that the mythmakers of Christianity hijacked for all their rituals. Mithras god of grain, wine, life springing from the underworld. Cultured life. That's so not Baphomet. Baphomet is sunshine falling on bright green leaves, insects buzzing past your ear, birds shouting in the sky overhead, stags crashing through the bushes, worms slithering up and down their tunnels, moss spreading across banks, jaguars stealthily moving in the rainforest, fish shooting the rapids on their irresistible drive to return home, sea anemones waving tentacles, fungi shifting vast quantities of nutrition from soil to tree, painted humans carrying baskets to gather food, caddis fly larvae sticking stones onto themselves, birds migrating across the globe in search of the best place to dine; organisms doing their own thing in their own places.

Baphomet and Mithras. One etymology (a highly dubious one) is Father Mithras; if so then Baphomet, father of Mithras, makes him older, first. How can a god be named after his son?

As the twentieth century progressed, we saw a tendency to want to live in houses with big windows, with links to the outside (the garden as 'another room'), even houses with fold-back walls, or built to allow living practically outside on the wide covered verandas (e.g. Ben Law's iconic temple to timber). It struck me; does this embody a turning towards the desire to live with Baphomet, after thousands of years in the cave dwellings of Mithras? And what would that mean?

If we've spent all this time, living in the psychological dark places shut away from the living world, where only shaman-warriors should spend much time, has this messed with our heads in a bad way? A whole population exposed to the trials of separation from the sunlit world for long periods of time, without the training or predilection for doing so, would go insane.

Imagine a religion built on a cult following of dedicated warriors, with trials of endurance and harsh teachings about the ways of death. As a central world myth for soldiers, this is a good strategy. But then think, what if this escaped under the guise of normal mass religion? The same basic shape to the stories told, the psychological structures built up from the physical activation of neurons, by entrance into the cave like temples lit by flames, to gaze on icons of the dead god (who rises again), filled with smoke and soaring walls to emphasise the tiny scale of the individual in the greater body of the church. Does that make for a healthy balanced mindset, if everyone gets this as core Reality? The body of the god is consumed, the blood is drunk, because it has a powerful symbolism for the initiated priest to become one with the god, to let him live again through the new bodies formed from death. But what if everyone does these trivial actions without the teachings of the deeper meanings? Without initiation? What would that do to a city's populace? To a country's population?

The shaman that I embody feels deep concern about these peoples. That the world I live in has descended from them, gives me a whole life's work and then some. I take strength from the fact that I do not act alone; living as a practitioner of group magick, and as a shaman with links to many other people of power, does allow for rapid dissemination of ideas, through personal contacts, magickal means, and in this day and age electronic media to transmit to a wider community than merely my immediate physical environment. Thank goddesses!

The Magical Conspiracy

The story that played out in the early 14th century for the Templars followed a well-worn groove. In 186BC Rome took action against the cult of Bacchus, another group accused of wild rites and secret oaths. Thousands of people were arrested and many executed. The implication was then, as it is now, that such a cult inflicts an injury on the body politic wherein radicalism and revolution may fester.

Nero did much the same in AD64, ordering his troops to storm Christian temples and break up their seditious love feasts. His methods of public executions included being torn apart by wild dogs, crucifixions and the innovative use of live human torches to illuminate the royal gardens at night.

Later the Christian Emperor Valens got his turn in the great sorcery persecution of 370AD. Anyone with connections to magical enterprises was tried on suspicion of high treason. As well as destroying his enemies Valens saw to it that whole libraries were incinerated, books of magic being considered almost as dangerous as magicians themselves.

The legal basis of the Templar trial was that of heresy by way of idolatry. The accusations themselves were formally delivered through Guilliaume de Norgaret, a nasty self-righteous hypocrite (he had been excommunicated by Pope Benedict XI and remained under censure throughout his prosecution of the Templars). The climate of the times was ripe for Norgaret's virtuous hatred of all things magical.

Allegations of sorcery were rapidly becoming a favourite stratagem for the courtiers of King Philip of France when jockeying for position. In 1308 the Bishop of Troyes was accused of causing the death of Queen Jeanne by baptising and impaling a wax image. Norgaret got all excited and added the crimes of sodomy and blasphemy to the charge sheet. The poor Bishop, who avoided execution by languishing in prison for years until the affair could be quietly forgotten, was also accused of usury. These strands of money lending, magic, heresy and treason were also twisted together into the noose around the neck of the Poor Knights.

Friday the thirteenth 1307 sees the beginning of the end. Agents acting for the French King arrest every member of the Templars they can get their hands on. The charge is one of heresy. The royal letter says of the Templars "...they have abandoned God their maker and sacrificed to demons...insane folk given over to the worship of idols". Baphomet, it seems, had been fingered. Although instigated by Philip the Fair the new weakling Pope, Clement V, was eventually forced to endorse the legality of the action. The wildfire spreads, with arrests occurring across Christendom. The Papal bull *Pastoralis Praeeminentiae* ordered all Christian monarchs in Europe to arrest the Templars and seize their assets. Most didn't need to be told twice.

In 1312 Clement V officially dissolved the Order. By 1314 the Grand Master of the Templars, Jacques de Molay, who had confessed under torture, retracted his statement. Geoffrey de Charney, Preceptor of Normandy, followed suit and protested his innocence. Declared guilty of being relapsed heretics, they were sentenced to burning alive at the stake in Paris on March 18, 1314. Accounts from the time claim that De Molay remained defiant to the end, asking to be tied that he might face his beloved Notre Dame Cathedral. The legend is that, as the flames blossomed around him, he screamed that Pope Clement and King Philip would soon meet their judgement before God. Pope

Clement died only a month later, and King Philip died in a hunting accident before the end of the year.

Almost 400 years later an altar to the horned god Cernunnos was discovered in the foundations of Notre Dame. Typical of the Templar story, the web weaves itself together through chance association, synchronicity, magic.

With the ringleaders out of the way Templars who had managed to evade arrest were pretty much forgotten about. Some joined the other major military Order The Knight Hospitallers of St. John, some legged it to territories safe for the excommunicated, such as Scotland or Switzerland.

For our literal Templars the show was over. Meanwhile the seed of the narrative, nourished in the dark of their secret ceremonies, was growing. The fire of the executions might have been put out, but it had lit the fuse on the myth of Templarism. The story of Baphomet was just beginning.

Ishtar goddess of war and sex. Baphomet god of death and life. Today's world worships one side but not the other, influenced by centuries of a god portrayed as a tortured dying icon. Where is the sacred veneration of sex, the creative principle, in our modern world?

Templars as knights of monasticism and war. Life and death. Without monocultural allegiance to either one or the other, they represented a mix between the vows of care and destruction. Yet their care was not allowed to extend into the realm of bodily pleasure; celibacy as with other monastic creeds was avowed. So do they mark a turning away from flesh in a Gnostic fashion? Or do the reports of their orgiastic rites hold truths of this repressed side emerging in caves?

Underground... It's all very Mithraic if you ask me. Or cave bear cult. Or north east Atlantic coast megalithic fake cave temple. Or the caves at Lascaux. Or the acoustic rooms of South America. Or the rooms of Turkey entered through tiny holes in walls. Or Finnish shamanic dwellings entered through roof doors. Or Mesoamerican adobes entered from the above. Or the church of Christ, entered through a ladder down into the ground. Or... hang on, a theme is glaring us in the face here. What is this obsession with underground chambers? Acoustic resonances? Symbolism of entering the earth? Entering the source of life, the destination of death?

Are we seeing here a semiotic fusion of the conceptual 'duality' of above/below- the earth, underworld where bodies are destined to descend, aboveworld where souls live eternally? While on the surface we live and die both. Baphomet as deity of the biosphere, locates firmly on this surface amongst us and around us. As deity of the dual, sHe unites the dichotomies of existence as a non-dual phenomenon. No wonder sHe defies depiction as either sex, or even as any species! Beyond paradox.

Intercession. Priests are allowed to petition god in two of the three Abrahamic religions (in Judaism the question of asking righteous individuals to pray for one is seen by many to interfere with the direct relation of the individual with their god, and Rabbis advise and officiate rather than pray for).

Caves. Totally dark. Unless manmade light is taken inside them. Our sense deprived optic nerves invent flashes, or entheogenic lights fill the mind's eye. Like Plato's cave, which we live in until the Mysteries reveal a world beyond, the cave metaphor must be an age-old powerful physical representation of the state of ignorance we inhabit until we are borne into the new daylight of awareness.

The Mystery religion of Baphomet then, the Circle of Baphomet, what's that about? No caves here. Where does the light flood into? The cave of the skull, the Golgotha of each individual consciousness.

The light we see by flashes in from all sides as we look into the eyes of our fellow travellers, and recognise the underground connectedness of Life. No man, after all, is an island.

The Inheritors of Baphomet

The Knights Templar may have been guilty of creating a State within a State. Quite probably they were on their way to creating their own mystery cult which, even if it wasn't actually heretical when they were apprehended, in time probably would have been. The effect of the Templar arrests, and the dissolution of the Order, was a significant one. A parallel today might be to imagine incarcerating all the members of the commercial banking sector. Church, Crown and the remaining Military Orders came howling into the power vacuum that was left. The Templars became 'the disappeared'. But had they really gone or had they merely been, metaphorically and perhaps literally, driven underground?

Did they or the heresy they perchance embodied persist, and if so who are their descendents?

From a conventional historical perspective the answer is simple; no one. However the myth of the Templars has been grafted onto vigorous stock. So much so that almost anyone who is anyone in the western esoteric scene today can count the Knights Templar as cultural ancestors.

Freemasons, Satanists, Thelemites, Wiccans and Chaos Magicians all name check the Poor Knights in their lineages. So what aspects of the Templars do these modern esotericists claim kinship with? The answer is that these groups see in the Templars a mysterious organisation with an initiatory tradition, one that was in possession of arcane knowledge. And at the core of this way of interpreting the Templars is their rich symbolic legacy, including their idol Baphomet.

Freemasonry, as the best known of these clandestine groups, has the iconography of Solomon's Temple at its heart. Predictably the origins of the Freemasons are obscure; there are hints of their existence as early as the 14th century. Freemasonry has many faces. On the one hand it is a proto-typical gentleman's club, however it also maintains distinctly occult credentials. Certainly by the 16th century we have Scottish Freemasons describing the esoteric practice of the Art of Memory (a cunning set of cognitive techniques ideal for both Qabalists and card sharks).

In 1646 the polymath Elias Ashmole becomes a Freemason. In 1672 he writes sympathetically about the Templars in his descriptions of another secret cultus the Order of the Garter (which the witch Doreen Valiente hypothesises was a Royal coven).

Easy with those witches, we'll meet them later

Ashmole shows marked interest in Rosicrucianism as well as emerging forms of natural science such as botany and astronomy. He translates the alchemical writings of Arthur Dee (John Dee's son). 1652 sees him publish his most important alchemical work, *Theatrum Chemicum Britannicum*. This volume compiles material, much of which had been preserved in privately held manuscripts. He founds the first university museum and in 1660, is a co-founder of the Royal Society of London for the Improvement of Natural Knowledge. The Royal Society grows in the same ontological soil in which Elias cultivates his investigations of magic and ceremony. This Society was to become the spearhead of Natural Philosophy, which was one of the most radical ideas to emerge into culture ever. This idea had been brewing for thousands of years in a series of secret traditions that had been a consistent, though sometimes deeply hidden strand, within western thought. For

Ashmole, the Templars were resonant with that current. They, along with the Gnostics, and the Hermeticists, were sects that had preserved this hidden knowledge: The knowledge of the process of first-hand exploration and revelation that today we name 'science'.

Ashmole's Royal Society was the formalisation of secret associations that had existed prior to it; groups such as The Invisible College. College members included Robert Boyle (chemist), John Wilkins (polymath), John Wallis (cryptographer), Christopher Wren (architect), William Petty (economist). In addition to the occasional meeting The Invisible College existed as a network of intellectuals, covertly swapping books with mushrooming marginalia as each reader added their observations and ideas. A hidden web of interactions that socially networked the most brilliant minds of the 17th century together. A Rosicrucian conspiracy carrying the scientific-gnostic heresy from dog-eared page to page, from mind to mind.

Several luminaries of The Invisible College became founding members of the Royal Society, the organisation that finally allowed this network of Invisibles to appear in public. Attempting to restore England's fortunes after the disastrous civil war this crown-backed think tank would help put the country back on its feet.

The beliefs of Royal Society were deeply indebted to philosopher and statesman Francis Bacon who died a few decades earlier.

> "Men have sought to make a world from their own conception and to draw from their own minds all the material which they employed, but if, instead of doing so, they had consulted experience and observation, they would have the facts and not opinions to reason about, and might have ultimately arrived at the knowledge of the laws which govern the material world."

Bacon (continuing the work of his much earlier namesake Roger Bacon, one of the first European advocates of empiricism) developed an investigative approach to knowledge we now call the scientific method. An influential statesman, lawyer and philosopher, like Ashmole, it is probable that Bacon was a Freemason. Writing in his *New Atlantis* Bacon describes a utopian culture in which "generosity and enlightenment, dignity and splendour, piety and public spirit" would shine through. Moreover he imagined a university where both pure and applied sciences would be studied. His ideal college was to be called Solomon's House. His perfect State was to be ruled over by the Rosicrucians.

It is to Bacon we owe the axiom 'knowledge is power'.

Natural Philosophy, what today we call science, was the critical mass lurking in the centre of the alchemists' laboratory. It really was the Universal Solvent, the Philosopher's Stone. And the key message of this Philosophy?

"Nullius in Verba" The Motto of the Royal Society "on the words of no one" Or "Think for yourself and question authority." Timothy Leary (paraphrasing Socrates).

In what way did Natural Philosophy, this science, challenge the status quo?

Christianity (as many of the other religions from that aeon) is a religion of The Book. During the medieval period knowledge was defined as What Had Been Written. And it wasn't just Biblical text that was considered to be, well, Gospel. Let's take an example from the same period that Ashmole is setting up the Royal Society.

William Harvey (born 1578 – died 1657) was a brilliant medic. Physician to both King James I and Charles I, he was fascinated with an experimental approach to medicine. Like all qualified doctors of the age he had successfully graduated as a medic by memorising and, on command regurgitating, the writings of Galen of Pergamum, the ancient Greek physician. Galen had written extensively on anatomy and physiology, logic and philosophy and it was his work that formed the theoretical and much of the practical application of medicine in both Christendom and the Islamic world. Harvey knew that Galen provided detailed descriptions of the movement of both venous and arterial blood, identifying each as having distinct and separate functions. Harvey, who liked tinkering with body parts through practices like dissection and vivisection, realised that Galen was, to put it simply, wrong. It took being the most famous and respected physician in the land, with an illustrious track record behind him before Harvey could stand up and give voice to what other physicians undoubtedly knew. Emperor Galen was in fact naked. The profession's knowledge was faulty. Worse, the implications were that the scholasticism of medieval philosophy was flawed. Medical knowledge had been based on almost exclusively on Galen's work. Galen, it was assumed, must be right because he is a Greek from the European Golden Age. His was an ancient text and therefore an authority because human knowledge was to be derived from trusted scholastic sources. Learning in medieval Europe was about marrying Classical philosophy with Christian texts and, through resolving the apparent (and indeed numerous) contradictions between these writings, one could come to understand the world. That was how one discovered the Truth, not grubbing around in the chest cavities of dying dogs.

(Ibn al-Nafis, the 13th century Middle Eastern anatomist was already wise to the truth about the functioning of the cardiovascular system. Perhaps the Templars found out about his work during their time in the Holy Land. Knowing the facts about how the heart works would have surely provided a great advantage in battlefield medicine.)

There is a shudder here, as we realise that the medieval universe is collapsing. (And indeed the literalism implicit throughout much

Christian thought.) We'd assumed that the Ancients were always right. What then if our own sense, our own experience, proves them wrong? We're going to need to experiment – with literally everything - to discover what is true. And we're going to start taking all those ancient writings with a pinch of salt. Even perhaps the Bible.

The Natural Philosophers were the experimenters. They were the alchemists, the antiquarians, the astrologers, the physicians and the magicians. They began to turn their back on the idea of holy infallible writ and instead chose a different course. They would be gnostics in the sense of seeking direct knowledge of God. They would do this by exploring the Book of Nature. The observable realm, the universe itself, would be their teacher. Clearly this is heresy, undoubtedly the slippery slope towards

Atheism

Idolatry

Paganism

(Baphomet)

The magician stands in the circle. The circle defines the universe and here he is God. He defines the initial conditions of the space and performs operations in that space according to a blend of inspiration and ceremonial formula. In this space he gains knowledge, discovers treasure.

The scientist stands in her laboratory. The laboratory defines the universe and here she is God. She defines the initial conditions of the space and performs operations in that space according to a blend of inspiration and accepted formula. In this space she gains knowledge, discovers treasure.

This similarity is not a coincidence.

The secret wisdom that Bacon, Ashmole and many others imagined was the wisdom of experience. It was the revelation that only through direct relationship with the world, through experiment, could truth really be discovered. In common with alchemical thinking, this process of understanding the Book of Nature, of discerning each link in the great Chain of Being, was both an inner and outer process. As the Natural Philosopher investigated the world, so he investigated God and himself. To read directly the laws of God, to see the works of His hand by personal observation, was the explicit aim of these men.

As above, so below

The stakes during this period in history were high. Monk-turned-heretic Giordano Bruno (1548–1600), argued that a change in humanity's perception of the heavenly order would cause changes in the social order. He argued that if heliocentricity (as one of the great discoveries of the dawning discourse of natural philosophy) could be established it would usher in a new age of Hermetic enlightenment. This enlightenment would include radical religious change throughout Christendom. Heliocentrism was only the visible aspect of radical religious change that Bruno was openly promulgating. As above, so below – as we learnt to read the heavens in a new way so a new fusion of Christianity and Paganism would arise. Obviously there were some people, notably the Pope, who didn't much care for this kind of suggestion. After travelling widely through Europe and setting up his own secret society (The Giordanisti) to promote his views Bruno was arrested by the Inquisition. He was imprisoned for eight years, before being burned at the stake in 1600. Cardinal Roberto Bellarmino presided over his trial and execution. Sixteen years later he would be the man who handed Galileo an order not to 'hold or defend' the heliocentric theory of Copernicus.

Men gathered in secret cabals such as the Invisible College to explore these ideas together. Secrecy was necessary because experimental investigations were inherently dissenting and certainly many of the results that turned up, like Harvey's re-interpretation of the circulatory system, flew in the face of accepted opinion. Members were probably mindful of Galileo's house arrest in 1634 for championing the heliocentrism of Copernicus.

Secrecy was also required because these men knew that they really were gaining privileged knowledge and the acquisition of that knowledge was intrinsically linked to an idea of elite spiritual development (remember; 'knowledge is power').

Many of the leading thinkers of any time inevitably hold positions of responsibility in their communities; often these roles involve assuming the practices of whatever religious persuasion holds sway. Consorting openly with those of different faith risked easy criticisms from one's close rivals. Royal Society meetings required strict adherence to a Science Only discussion policy, matters of political and religious tenor were forbidden. Sounds familiar…

Secrecy was necessary because some of the techniques required for philosophical investigations were ones that might be frowned on by the Crown, the Church and the people. Better to Keep Silence about the nature of one's experimental work than to wind up with the population of the town storming your laboratory with pitchforks and burning torches.

So embedded within 17th century Masonic style organisations we have an increasing number of men who are guarding (and covertly promoting) a genuine hidden wisdom. Moreover this is a wisdom that can be reasonably be argued is of some antiquity – namely the thirst to discover unmediated knowledge. Natural philosophy and experimental method is the Promethean approach, stealing the fire from heaven. This is gnostic personal revelation through direct experience. This is the theurgic ritual, with the aim of henosis, the goal of uniting with the divine source of all. Such a process does not require a priesthood to intercede on one's behalf. Rather it is conducted alone, or in small clandestine groups.

(The Brothers are doing it for themselves)

This secret wisdom makes more and more inroads into culture. As indeed does the practice of mystery cult initiation. By the 19th century literally millions of people are initiates of the Masons and similar groups. In 1859 the effects of Natural Philosophy deliver a body blow to the scholastic approach and the hegemony of Divine Scripture. Charles Darwin publishes '*On the Origin of Species by Means of Natural Selection, or The Preservation of Favoured Races in the Struggle for Life*'. The Baphomet is out of the bag – the truth seems to be that man is, in fact, an animal. One of many forms of life and not the unique image of God on earth.

Four years earlier the French occultist Eliphas Levi visited Britain where he met the novelist and playwright Edward 'the pen is mightier than the sword' Bulwer-Lytton. (Lytton would later go on to write the influential science fiction novel *The Coming Race* about a civilisation of subterranean supermen. This culture is powered by 'vril', the root from which the brand name Bovril is derived.) Bulwer-Lytton was fascinated by Rosicrucianism and encouraged Lévi to write an esoteric treatise. This was published in 1855 as *Dogme et Rituel de la Haute Magie*, and was translated into English by Golden Dawn adept Arthur Edward Waite as *Transcendental Magic, its Doctrine and Ritual*. The book opens with these lines:

> "Behind the veil of all the hieratic and mystical allegories of ancient doctrines, behind the darkness and strange ordeals of all initiations, under the seal of all sacred writings,

Fig 2 Baphomet, from Eliphas *Levi's Dogme et Rituel de la Haute Magie*

in the ruins of Nineveh or Thebes, on the crumbling stones of old temples and on the blackened visage of the Assyrian or Egyptian sphinx, in the monstrous or marvellous paintings which interpret to the faithful of India the inspired pages of the Vedas, in the cryptic emblems of our old books on alchemy, in the ceremonies practised at reception by all secret societies, there are found indications of a doctrine which is everywhere the same and *everywhere carefully concealed.*"

It is from this book that we have the most famous image of Baphomet. A hybrid human beast, the key to The Mystery. Human and animal combined.

Enlightenment

It all started with alchemy. My first chemistry lesson at university, a foundation year; our introduction to science explained how science only provides us with a model of reality. 'Atoms' are not real in an objective way; there are no small spheres whizzing around at the heart of everything. It's only a story. Science provides us with ides, hypotheses, with which we take hold of matter, and manipulate it. If the idea works we keep it, whilst striving for a better one… A basic principle of creative thinking, states that you continue searching for another, better solution, even after finding one. Alchemists started the testing of ideas. Because they were so intent on genuinely reaching their goal of the transformation of base metals into gold, they took the instruction texts history gave them and tested if they worked. And when they didn't they tried to see why, by adaptation, by refinement, by starting over again, by blowing themselves up a la *Discworld* archetypal narrative causality.

They began the move towards questioning received knowledge in an open, overt, fundamentally observable manner. They kept records, they developed ways of methodology that Francis Bacon would later formalise as the Scientific Method.

This first science lesson took place in the Hall, once the Big House of the area, a small manorial dwelling. Now part of the university, it houses the Law School and spill-over lessons from the main teaching rooms.

But does this new method of sticking to literal truth itself offer the only solution to the errors of slavishly following mistaken books?

Have we thrown out any babies with the long cold bathwater? Could there be a further solution to discover?

We, Here & Now, live in the rational world. The world of reliable measures, of Laws of Nature, where arational thought has respect only when circumscribed as Art or another dismissible category irrelevant to the daily grind.

Why? Historically we can point a finger at The Enlightenment, the dawn of scientific thinking. Transport ourselves back to that time and place; superstitious preachings from Mother Church abound, bizarre folk customs dictating society's conduct. A need for a less passionate, more verifiable mode of decision-making needs to arise. Enter Science, with The Royal Society acting as a common ground for people from all religions, classes, and backgrounds, to meet and discuss a topic with a blank page, starting from observation of reality instead of ancient writings.

They needed to turn their backs on visions and voices, look at numbered certainties amidst a sea of ritualised stagnant ceremonies. Without this move our world would not have achieved a realistic view of How Things Work. However… this focus on the rational to the exclusion of all else has left us damaged. Our task now centres on ways of revaluing the arational, as a qualitatively essential perspective. Restricting value to numbered quantities results in money choices ruling our lives to the cost of understanding other values, some of which mean more to us, as animals.

Isaac Newton, mathematically obsessed with counting everything, presided over the Royal Society for over 20 years. Without his autistic preoccupation with graphs and measuring quantity, perhaps the qualitative measures of his contemporaries would have developed a statistical method of representation, and today's science would appear very different. Many of the early members of the Royal Society, such as Sir Humphrey Davy, kept beautifully subjective whilst accurate observational records. If this first person approach had continued, the world today might look quite different. As it is, the subjective vanished from respectable science for a few centuries there, reappearing now as the social studies decided to acquire respectability; graphs and charts derived from qualitative data now made feasible with the vast number crunching computational devices we have on every desk. Metrics for comparing happiness, ordinal values, even a few raw statements from interviewees make themselves visible and have import in this expanded awareness that quantitative numbers might not capture the full picture after all. (At which, Newton spins in his grave at a precise speed, while Davy looks down from heaven with the angels and smiles.)

We have been fed the axiom that any Malleable truth = deceptive, untrue. Only immutable truths have a place in an unchanging society with an eternal, unquestionable status quo. Christianity (or rather the Holy Roman Empire's version of it, as represented officially these days by the Catholic Church, and less formally by those Good Christian folk in positions of power held by virtue of simple tradition) excludes or strictly defines the parameters of ecstatic states, lest they contradict interpreted scripture on how to interact with the Holy Spirit. The process of civilization puts breaks on our wilderness and wildness. But, paradigms only flourish as they support contemporaneous workable systems of energy gathering and distribution. The time has come for a radical shift from the past systems, and with technological developments this is inevitable. While we try out different means of alternative fuel and resource supply, we need to have a belief system which allows for temporarily functioning truths; today, we will think wind power has value, tomorrow, solar cells might prove better…

I believe that in a permissive cultural context a society of human animals requires entheogens as part of the daily (and historical) scale proper functioning and development of that culture. Creativity and inspiration of all types of technology and craft has always relied upon what we have been calling ASC for their fullest expression. Entheogens form a deep rooted time tested access point to these states. Behaviourally induced ASCs can also work although these can prove trickier to enter.

Whether used widely or by certain role affiliated individuals, a culture without the neophilia these various substances/behaviours induce, is doomed to fossilise and stagnate.

Just as the technological harnessing of fuels allowed slaves to achieve emancipation, current advances in energy/information gathering and delivery promise to allow emancipation of 'states of consciousness' other than linear rationalism, and then, freed from the machine world of coal and clockwork, thinking outside the square box can flourish once more, with ineffable unguessable results. A spiral of escalating insights and enthusiasm may well occur, driving efficient and aesthetically impressive solutions to the challenges we face in this '21st' century.

We turn now to the old story of Nature, red in tooth and claw.

The male of the species fights, or displays marvellous colouring in order to win the right to sire offspring.

Ha, yeah.

From here, I can see that the early naturalists were, in main, ex-military men. Like archaeologists of the 19th century, they saw hillforts, fights and splendid uniforms winning hearts and giving prestige.

However.

They did not make notes of those unremarkable occurrences, the long hours waiting for something to happen, when life just drifts on

– the background hum of co-existence and facilitation, the mutual symbiosis (either direct or via environmental alteration) that any biome mostly consists of.

They did not write about the female of the species having to develop ever more selective desires, aligned with accurate signals of genetic fitness, to choose the male she would allow to sire her offspring.

To be fair those early thinkers often didn't have the knowledge or equipment necessary to detect some of this, but I suspect even if they had they would have remained blind to that outside their own world.

Today, trade models rule archaeological visionaries, and biology has two scales, cellular and population. Values, quantifiable exchange and growth, make nice graphs. Beyond the numbers there be dragons – ritual, behaviour, ungeneralisable processes impossible for any external observer to examine 'scientifically'. They do not count.

Hard facts, the Enlightenment decided, were all that mattered. The superstitious nonsense of arcane religion was clearly ridiculous, and needed to be dismissed, they held to a revolutionary theory that God's laws could be read direct from experience, not rely on the dusty words of long dead ancients. Hard evidence to justify decision making and the stories of How we Are.

Taking back the power of thinking for oneself from established authorities upsets more than a few apple carts, so they worked in secret under strict codes of limiting discussions, inviting individuals from divers backgrounds, and importantly persuading the king to give his patronage to this worthy mission. One suspects that freedom from religious tyranny featured large in their mission statement.

Somewhere along the way, un-evidenced reality got lost, discarded and forgotten. Until recent technology and careful searches, the scant traces of food, cloth, baskets, leather work, feathers and braids, elements of our species tapestry for thousands of years, were as visible as the smoke of our forefathers' fires, telling us as much as the songs our great great grandmothers sang.

Of Caves and Spires

Back down in the cave. Specifically a cave in Royston, Hertfordshire, fifty miles north of London. Today the cave is accessed down a long tunnel that descends gradually, sloping towards the foot of the chamber. The cave itself is an artificial structure cut from the chalk that underlies this area. Its shape is vaguely conical, only a few metres wide at the base and tapering to a point towards the surface. High above the floor of the cave one can see the original entrance. This portal was cunningly hidden, as was the chimney from the space, which was vented through the hearth of the building that used to stand above it. When the cave was first created, sometime in the 14th century, visitors would have had to crawl into it through a small opening. They would have alighted onto a wooden platform shaped like a hexagram. To one side of the platform was a large burning cresset on a movable arm. Posable mood lighting for whatever went on there perhaps? A trap door through the wooden platform permitted access, via a ladder, to the base of the cave. Here an octagonal floor was created. Pillars holding the hexagram platform up were struck down into this eight-sided figure, their measurements and number recalling exactly the architecture of the Dome of the Rock. On one side of the lower chamber there is a recess of earth, foetus shaped but man sized, known as 'the grave'. All around the lower chamber are carvings. There are doves and knights and a scene of a man being burned at the stake along with the word 'trial'. There are abstract designs and symbols that, before the structure was abandoned, seem to have been deliberately excised. When the site was re-discovered in the 18th century it was found that the cave had been filled in with soft topsoil. In that area of England the topsoil is exceedingly thin. It would have taken many people, presumably working covertly, to seal the cave. Whoever did the work wanted to hide, but not destroy this mysterious cell.

Tiny cells deep within the earth, like those places in which life arose so very long ago. Places of secret conspiracy…

In a prominent position in the cave is a carving of Saint Catherine, a patron of Templars. This, along with what appears to be the scene showing Jacques de Molay being executed, suggests that whoever was using this cave were at least inspired by, if not the direct cultural descendants of the Templars. Why Saint Catherine? Perhaps because she is the Christian counterpart to the Pagan Hypatia, the brilliant and martyred scholar of Alexandria. The archetypal Wise Woman.

Who used this place hidden beneath the earth, at the exact intersection of two ancient Roman roads? Whatever they were up to was certainly a dangerous business. This was undoubtedly a nest for heretics. (An equivalent modern term, which is as emotive to us as 'heretic' was to people in the Middle Ages, would be 'paedophile ring'.) But the building that existed above the site would have afforded some protection. It was occasionally used as a hunting lodge. A place where men from many different backgrounds could meet and stay the night without arousing suspicion. From their Lodge our guests would have descended into the subterranean space, perhaps into an initiated tradition.

Look amongst the carvings and you can see the symbols of early Freemasonry.

So no connection between the Templars and the Masons? The hands that carved Royston Cave would beg to differ.

Humans mark out space; we are architects, masons of our reality. And we can see the tensions in that reality only too well. Consider, as only one example among many, the tension between the Gothic and the Classical. On the one hand we have the ancient Temples of the classical world and Egypt. These are mimicked by many great civic buildings; The Bank of England, The British Museum and the Washington Memorial. Then there is the Gothic; the medieval cathedrals of Europe and later The Natural History Museum in London. Time and again these psychic themes are thrown up in stone. The Dome of the Rock, reflected deep down in the architecture of Royston Cave becomes Capitol Hill and Saint Paul's Cathedral in London.

From our caves we elaborate our psychic spaces, building our temples according to motifs that are deeply ingrained in us.

Age old wisdom

Earth celebrates her 4.5 billionth anniversary about now. 4,500,000,000 journeys around the sun, that giant ball of hydrogen and helium, so massive that atoms fuse together at its core, the photons taking thousands of years to reach the outer levels, from where flames larger than our planet flare into space, and the antique light particles (or waves...) embark on a final journey through space taking 8 minutes to reach your eye. At last we know the material that burns so brightly; once, coal was suggested as fuel, and a helpful Victorian scholar calculated how heavy the star, and how long the fire would keep burning. Like the efforts to construct accurate plans of the Ark, we scoff at the puny stories those folks of old told themselves in order to describe the world.

Let's go back a short step in time to the 19th century C.E. Science has explored the age of the earth, and begun to divine a way of explaining how the multiplicity of life forms upon it might have evolved. Philosophically, we have started to see ways of conceptualising the unity of diversity, as our cultures and individuals spread to other territories en masse, in search of Other spiritual visions; the utopian movements of the early American settlers, wanting to practise their doctrine-free forms of worship, set up small colonies and projects in that vast continent.

In their quest for alternative paths to God, they encounter the native beliefs of The Great Spirit as a nature god, imminent in every stone and brook; refreshingly absent of book larnin', this view strikes a chord with many intellectuals and religious thinkers. The Reverend

Alcott, as well as the Thoreau family, embrace this creed with open arms, though subtly. Their daughter and son create works that still inspire today; more importantly the inspirations gained from this vision of God as the Spirit of Wilderness changed the face of the earth both locally and subsequently across all continents, a process very much alive and ongoing for ecologists today.

Age old wisdom

Earth celebrates her 4.5 billionth anniversary about now. 4,500,000,000 journeys around the sun, that giant ball of hydrogen and helium, so massive that atoms fuse together at its core, the photons taking thousands of years to reach the outer levels, from where flames larger than our planet flare into space, and the antique light particles (or waves...) embark on a final journey through space taking 8 minutes to reach your eye. At last we know the material that burns so brightly; once, coal was suggested as fuel, and a helpful Victorian scholar calculated how heavy the star, and how long the fire would keep burning. Like the efforts to construct accurate plans of the Ark, we scoff at the puny stories those folks of old told themselves in order to describe the world.

Let's go back a short step in time to the 19th century C.E. Science has explored the age of the earth, and begun to divine a way of explaining how the multiplicity of life forms upon it might have evolved. Philosophically, we have started to see ways of conceptualising the unity of diversity, as our cultures and individuals spread to other territories en masse, in search of Other spiritual visions; the utopian movements of the early American settlers, wanting to practise their doctrine-free forms of worship, set up small colonies and projects in that vast continent.

In their quest for alternative paths to God, they encounter the native beliefs of The Great Spirit as a nature god, imminent in every stone and brook; refreshingly absent of book larnin', this view strikes a chord with many intellectuals and religious thinkers. The Reverend

Alcott, as well as the Thoreau family, embrace this creed with open arms, though subtly. Their daughter and son create works that still inspire today; more importantly the inspirations gained from this vision of God as the Spirit of Wilderness changed the face of the earth both locally and subsequently across all continents, a process very much alive and ongoing for ecologists today.

Deep ecology

So how did this come about, this occult blending of a Judaeo-Christian godform with the Native American Great Spirit under the guise of observer methods from the scientific method? The climate of spiritual belief in Europe, and England in particular, by this time lacked a central figure that had any kind of credence. God seemed to have deserted us as a living presence, as Blake lamented in so many of his poems. Other poets, notably Wordsworth and Coleridge, deplored the horrendous state of a society that treated people so mechanically and without dignity. How could the leaders of this society, they asked, claim to have any kind of link to a loving god and allow poverty and cruelty to exist? How could a church maintain any kind of following while it stamped on the life embracing desires of its members as wrong? By asking these questions publicly, articulating the private thoughts of their readers, a space was created into which a new God could appear.

The Enlightenment had gone too far, scientific measurement criteria exterminating the invisible God whose divine plans and mathematical beauty their studies were meant to glory in.

By retreating from the horror of the industrial landscape of the English landscape, by finding awe and spiritual ecstatic visions in those places beyond the reach of man, they and their contemporaries such as John Clare, found their god in nature, beneath the vaulted skies.

Across the water in America the poems of these social writers were read, and the poets written to and even visited, by the families of

New Conchord, a post-Utopian town with a strong connection to the local people's more animistic belief systems.

They saw the link; they lived in a potentially ideal situation where the land still thrived with natural life, whilst they built European style houses in towns in the very midst of this new Eden. The works of literature they created, such as *Walden; or, Life in the Woods* and *Little Women*, spoke of a world where people fitted within the natural scheme of things, where God was to be sought in contemplation of rain, animals and a closer relationship with the non-human, by transcending the prescriptions of holy scriptures and literature, by choosing how one lives in a deliberate, aware and awake manner.

The American Transcendentalist movement has had an enormous effect on the physical world. By promoting the idea of Wilderness as spiritual retreat, a cultural climate existed where the proposal to set aside large areas from which humans were to be excluded (except for temporary expeditions into the primordial world of the unspoilt), was met with enthusiasm and acceptance. The National Parks system of the USA was inspired by the legacy of the Transcendentalists' perspective. The cathedrals of the New World, the favourite places of spiritual worship and pilgrimage, manifest as canyons and rock formations, free from the touch of human hands.

Thoreau and Emerson stand out as the eminent voices of this group, however the wider cultural impact of the coming together of American Utopian descendants with the Native American philosophies of the Great Spirit inherent in all Life, crept inexorably through many areas of Western literature and even science. Wilderness provides sanctuary for a deity infused with gnostic ancestry, with the living breathing (and geological) world of Nature fused together, one that suggests our own Baphometic figure, save for one important species. *Homo sapiens*, inventor of machines and despair, pollution and inhumanity to his fellow creatures, does not have access to these modern Gardens of Eden, except as a temporary visitor and under specific restricted conditions. We may enter these hallowed places, to watch, learn and record, but never to partake or influence overtly the magical woods mountains and animals ring fenced by the legislation of the wild areas.

John Muir, a key figure in American wilderness movements such as the Sierra Club, was influenced by Emerson. His writings set up a tension between solitary experience of Spiritual Wilderness and materialist industrialism/mass humanity; for Muir, man is a bad animal.

Emerson's 'vivacious friend' Margaret Fuller, the first editor of the transcendentalist journal The Dial, had her own sphere of influence. Her most famous prodigy was her great-nephew, Buckminster Fuller, designer of the geodesic dome beloved of simpler living advocates the world over. He quoted her as saying "I must start with the universe and work down to the parts, I must have an understanding of it", words that shaped his own approach.

These few examples of personal connections and the way a network spreads its take on the world via various media, has since echoed through our culture in the design and construction of the internet. Stewart Brand, editor of the influential Whole Earth Catalogue, himself heavily indebted to Buckminster Fuller for inspiration during the early years of his career, provides a prominent link between the Transcendalists and today's vision of a world of 'mud huts with computers' that some of us yearn for. Earthships, cob buildings, and round houses, solar powered and linked to the global information superhighways, vibrant communities embedded within the land they grow from.

Brand's Whole Earth catalogue, first published in 1968, the year of this book's authors' births, shaped the culture of a major sector of America and other lands. The hippie communes attempted in the 70's wanted to return to the land, a simpler way of life, yet retaining useful technologies. They didn't quite get it right, as this way of life needs a strong element of rootedness in the groundwork of community, a genuine engagement with the local existing inhabitants, human as well as animal.

This is where the American Transcendentalists went seriously astray.

They saw Nature as a pristine wilderness, for people to visit, recharge, then return to the trials of civilised life. The creation of the National Parks concretised this philosophy; John Muir saved vast swathes of land from urban sprawl, it is true, but like the Town and Country planning act of the British Isles, separating out people from beautiful landscapes has left us alienated from our own place as one species amongst the others, a hang over from the biblical concept of humans as stewards lording it over a walled garden creation.

How many ordinary folk would identify themselves as natural? I fear, that most of us cannot help but define man-made and natural as entirely separate categories; this Us and Them approach lies at the root of so many societal ills, we must invest considerable endeavour towards removing this distinction.

Humans, bio-engineers par excellence, have altered their surroundings more than any other creature, and now we have interfered with the mechanisms of the Earth herself, we outstrip in our effects the very geological forces. Earth moving, water diversions, atmospheric composition, light and energy flows, on a planetary scale, show Homo sapiens as the major geological influence bar none.

Not only are we natural, we are now a true Force of Nature, greater than the giants of old, destroying mountains, moving rivers, altering the levels of the oceans, changing the air we breathe.

Yet we remain deeply unaware of this at a visceral level. Each of us individual organisms, one of seven billion, knows how insignificant we are. As intelligent consciousnesses we act on of what we see, what we know, of the immediate world. This result of our biological sensory input works for scattered groups of a hundred or so people, whose influence as animals with basic tools has limits. As a global group of seven billion, however, with massive mechanised tools utilising vast reserves of stored energy from the last billions of years, an individual acts with the power of thousands of animals, despite their intelligence remaining singular.

Decisions taken by individuals often make little sense from a wider perspective. Collectively we act in small discrete steps, summing to overall patterns without deliberate aim.

However, as I write this book, I can gain other views of this world I inhabit. I can press buttons, and a picture of the Earth appears, now so familiar to us since Stewart Brand's campaign for NASA to release the first photograph of our home planet from space. Further, I can zoom in, to any part, and see with my own eyes the surface of my world. More buttons take me to photographs taken by other individuals, showing me this world through their eyes. I can search for encyclopaedic knowledge on almost any topic I can imagine, and even more that I cannot. I can publish the most fleeting thought to an audience of hundreds immediately, who in turn may pass on my thoughts.

Collectively I identify with a population group of a couple of hundred or so individuals spread throughout the world. My sphere of influence remains a similar size to that of an individual of old, yet my group exists on more than one continent, overlapping with other groups with a far greater degree of intimacy than ever possible before.

My internalised version of Us, expands way beyond those I see in the flesh every day. I belong firmly to more than one group, cyber communities, physical world social networks, geographically based neighbourhoods. I travel often, staying with friends, so my home moves between nodes much as the seasonally determined semi nomadic way of life of my ancestors.

How does this kind of new lifestyle alter the ways in which we interact as a species? We can see as another sees, hear their words from continents away, share advice and experiences to prevent errors repeating, help successes spread rapidly without having to reinvent the wheel in each separate country. I like this. Yet, this doesn't go far enough. I'd like to expand our feeling of community, those we share our experiences of the world with, beyond humanity, into the other animals, the other plants, the bacteria, the fungi, all the kingdoms of Life. More than that, I would wish to see non human animals take advantage of our technologies, eventually a seamless flow of integrated communication between life, tools, and environment, the richest tapestry of all possible worlds.

Projects already exist to enable rudimentary forays into this expansion beyond the anthropocentric. Farmers can get numerical data on weather and soil conditions, displayed through interfaces of colour and human friendly graphics. Remote cameras set up in birds' nests, or even sensors attached to animals, show us what they see. More ambitious projects aim to allow for feedback from creatures other than human, or direct from the environment itself, turning buoys floating offshore into intelligent agents able to raise or lower harbour locks depending upon sea conditions. The world has started to control itself, via our tools. Thermostatic controls of fairly simple on off mechanisms now, will undoubtedly lead to more advanced ways of allowing controls on subtler levels.

Perhaps in future, an animal's presence could activate a road crossing sign or even barrier, so the traffic can stop. A species migrating through an area, in need of food, could alert the local caring humans to its plight, and have the appropriate meals awaiting it. Those needing water could have the local water mains linked to a tap activated to provide refreshment. Nanotechnology opens further avenues for mass decision making by groups of smaller creatures or other organisms. Sending information to either people, or an automatic response. Allowing the rest of the living world access to our tools, goes a long way to acquiring a true Baphometic level of pooled awareness, for our species and, theirs.

This process will contain errors, bumps and the inevitable misuse by those out to exploit. Personally I see it's emergence as inevitable, and that by linking in to our informational world the physical existence of other species, the atmosphere, the hydrosphere, and the geosphere too, we create conditions for true embodied consciousness of our world. Baphomet the deity exists as the combined spirit of all living things on our planet. Baphomet the egregore has begun to speak, through our human voices, art, movements. Baphomet the materialised living reality, can only begin to think and act collectively when the sense impressions of many inputs feed into hir ability to affect the physical world direct, instead of having to use our species as translators.

Artificial Intelligence researchers have started using the actions of robots to provide the AI with a sense of the outer world and how to handle it, analogous to the average infant creature crawling upon the face of the earth. This self-selection of appropriate algorithmic solutions from the world of movement, subsequently provides solutions to questions in the rarefied fields of intellect. Language follows physical constructs, beliefs and mental manipulations of information likewise. Any AI with a sense of empathy, must necessarily follow our steps along this road, understand from the very beginning it exists in a world that extends outside its skin.

Our greatest gift, the metaphor model of the world, the ability to see the world as an-other sees it, transforms a locally isolated population into an intrinsic functioning component of the planet, increasing chances of survival, more globally efficient use of resources, and amazing chances to interact with the external.

I suspect, that much of this future engineering for life will necessarily rely upon fairly straightforward mechanistic equipment, distributed network levels of decision-making; we have seen that centrally controlled networks tend to fail. Think steampunk at a near molecular scale.

Which is not to say that skills of a less obviously mechanistic type are now redundant, far from it! Integrating all these flows into a coherent shape requires the observer self to have developed considerable strength. Also, esoteric currents manifesting through our 21st century benefit from the magickal input as much as writing, chemistry and astronomy did in their day.

Practices we tend to group under that catch-all nebulous term 'spiritual' often increase our connections with our bodies. Different traditions utilise these sensations to different ends, some to transcend the sensorial world, others to enter it more fully; those who have walked this path more than a few steps, know that all paths tend to lead towards the non-dual, via different doors. As meditation, breath control, yoga, concentration, experimentation with brain states, responses to rhythms, allow us to feel our embedded natures as individuals within the matrix of lifeforms, we cannot help but start to feel the shared experience of other species beyond the walls of our man-made illusions.

Actions and motivations start with emotional knowledge. Intellect provides us with a place to reflect upon those actions subsequently, but we act upon gut feelings. Changing peoples' minds about how to live, only follows from changing people's feelings. The spiral of learning, as we feel, act, reflect, change our feelings, repeat; this cycle gives the key to what we do next. Magick provides techniques to hack the system, to prod it into a better functioning stable state.

Maintaining a still centre in the midst of the Chaos of the Normal we now produce, allows us to take decisions freed from the unthinking compulsions of our histories; the webs of Wyrd we each inhabit provide platforms to jump off from, the reality tunnels lead us here to the present where our choices spread out, waiting like The Seven Cups for us to grasp one firmly.

Fate, then, as envisioned by our ancestors, has less to do with destiny and more to do with perceiving patterns in the fabric of reality to develop as we see fit. Pick your colours, take up your tapestry bobbins, and get weaving!

As magicians, we have the resources of our predecessors' experience, often recorded in arcane literary survivals, sometimes apparent from the direct results of their workings. The decoding of symbols which occult study leads us to practice constantly can prove only helpful in a world increasingly using pictorial and meta structural information; the words of a text make up a material out of which soar towers of imagination, flowers of delight bloom, expected themes get subverted in order to elicit attention; as Directors of the film of our own lives, we can choose to use our own hands to place personal touches of golden threads to highlight the special moments, even while still utilising the punchcards of the mechanical loom programming for occasions when repetitive facsimiles have a better chance of success. Writing a complex text takes time and infinitely subtle moves coupled to focussed attention, eating a bowl of food takes reliable, consistent movements. Both ways of acting have a part to play...

That Discordian Conspiracy so far...

So the Illuminati, the magician priests of ancient Atlantis spread throughout the world. Covert and yet all penetrating, their machinations infecting every aspect of society. Mysterious and yet leaving an all too apparent trail of symbolic clues, pointing to their activity. The spider at the centre of the web.

From the assassination of the Emperor Julian through to the killing of JFK. THEY are the ones who are REALLY in control. The jewish-cabalistic-masonic-synarchist-revolutionary-libertarian-alchemical-neo-nazi-lizard-banking-megacorporation-underground…you get the idea.

This is the associative way of thinking. The blending together of concepts from droplets of thought. Frozen facts, flash-thawed by the amphetamine logic of the paranoid, the schizophrenic.

The magician.

Baphomet, as the key icon of the Templars, finds herself drawn into the political Left and Right, the popular, the avant-garde, even street culture. Baphomet is assuredly a key part of the conspiratorial network.

Down the years Baphomet is transformed from an improbable idol, a bearded head, into the insignia of the inverted pentagram. This is emblazoned in gold on the black t-shirt of a young man who walks through the streets of London. He doesn't know why he wears it. It's not Satan (he's savvy to the pagan idea of the horned god) and yet he secretly knows that it **is** Satan. It is something that stares out of the triangle, out of the pentagonal lattice and howls. Howls to emerge, to run amok in culture, to unleash a powerful force into our species. Beyond good and evil it simply is, it does.

Above me the street lamp flickers. We're waiting at Streatham station. My Dad has come to meet me. I've been to see the witches. Their home had snakes in it, and incense and magick. The High Priest of the coven, an affable man, sparkling with a showman's flair and a mercurial mind. He told me about his time in Grand Lodge, about the black and white chequered floor. He told me about the ceremonies and how they were very similar to those of Alexandrian Wicca.

The Masons who carried the Baphometic DNA dropped their payload into Wicca and Wicca is a primary root of the modern Paganism, a religious movement of tremendous vigour and creativity. A religion in which God is a beast. A horned beast.

Licking Baphomet into Shape

It was Joseph von Hammer-Purgstall, diplomat and polyglot, who began the process of giving Baphomet a more clearly defined form. In his essay *Mysterium Baphometis revelatum* he elaborated a fabulous history that claimed the Templars as Gnostic heretics. Hammer drew on material from the Grail romances to support his argument and referred to the alleged discovery in 1818 of four 'Baphomets', idols that had been housed in the Imperial Museum of Vienna. These heads, Hammer opined, represented the divinity of the Gnostics, named *Mété* (Wisdom).

Following Hammer's time, Levi imagines his properly occult Baphomet, describing the image adorning his Transcendental Magic, he writes;

> "The goat on the frontispiece carries the sign of the pentagram on the forehead, with one point at the top, a symbol of light, his two hands forming the sign of hermetism, the one pointing up to the white moon of Chesed, the other pointing down to the black one of Geburah. This sign expresses the perfect harmony of mercy with justice. His one arm is female, the other male like the ones of the androgyn of Khunrath, the attributes of which we had to unite with those of our goat because he is one and the same symbol. The flame of intelligence shining between his horns is the magic light of the universal balance, the image of the soul elevated above matter, as the flame, whilst being tied to matter, shines above it. The beast's head

expresses the horror of the sinner, whose materially acting, solely responsible part has to bear the punishment exclusively; because the soul is insensitive according to its nature and can only suffer when it materialises. The rod standing instead of genitals symbolises eternal life, the body covered with scales the water, the semi-circle above it the atmosphere, the feathers following above the volatile. Humanity is represented by the two breasts and the androgyny arms of this sphinx of the occult sciences..."

The Mendes tag is likely to have come from Herodotus of Halicarnassus (aka 'the father of history'). In his *Histories* Herodotus claims that the principle deity of Mendes, the Greek name for the Egyptian city of Djedet, was depicted as horned and with a goat's legs. Our ancient historian also claims that, during a public ritual, a woman would copulate with a goat in honour of the God. It seems that Levi blended this story (the actual Egyptian bovid was more likely to have been a ram) with the imagery that already existed of The Devil in the Tarot. For Levi the name Baphomet has a Qabalistic meaning, it is an anagram of the Latin TEM OHP AB - Templi omnium hominum pacis abbas "The Father Of The Temple Of Peace Of All Men". Levi naturally suggested that the Temple in question was that of King Solomon.

Levi's vision of Baphomet is a nexus of many ideas. The divine androgyne, the idea of divinity embedded in the world, the sanctity of the sexual force, alchemy, Qabalah and more. He also does that classic trick of inverting the established order. Whereas Hammer ranged against the idolatry of the Templars Levi makes the case that they were in fact worshipping the True God. The assumption of Levi was that the Gods of the old religion (ancient Paganism) became the devils of the new (Christianity). Therefore the newly emerging religious consciousness (which would later become modern Paganism) sought its new gods in hell. Levi looked at The Devil in the tarot

Fig 3   L'Azoth des Philosophes, Basil Valentine, 1659.

(initially a gaming deck and only later a tool for divination) and instead saw God.

We pass the tarot deck around the circle. A robed figure takes a card, shakes its head and then passes the cards on. We continue in this way until one of our number selects Atu XV – The Devil. They have been chosen to be the horse that will be ridden by Baphomet in the Mass of Chaos B.

Time to take a closer look at Levi's Baphomet. Let's examine our divine chimera piece by piece.

Some people say that Eliphas found his inspiration in the grotesque gargoyles of the Templar Commandry at Saint Bri le Vineux. Occultist and writer Michael Howard tells us;

> "The Gargoyle is in the form of a bearded horned figure with pendulous female breasts, wings and cloven feet. It sits in a crossed-legged position which resembles statues of the Celtic stag god, Cernnunnus or the Horned One, found in Gaul (France) before the Roman occupation."

So what does Levi say?

> "This is the AZOTH of the sages on its pedestal of Salt and Sulphur. The symbolic head of the Goat of Mendes is occasionally given to this figure, and then it is the Baphomet of the Templars and the Word of the Gnostics. 'universal medicine' or 'universal solvent'."

Fig 4 Alchemical Seal reproduced in Stanislas Klossowski de Rola *The Golden Game: Alchemical Engravings of the Seventeenth Century.*

Azoth is a word derived from the Arabic *al-zâ'ûq* "the mercury". Employed as an alchemical jargon, Azoth appears in a variety of arcane texts, for example, by German alchemist Johann Basil Valentine, *Azoth of the Philosophers*, published in 1659. Here Azoth is the perfected human. Azoth is the A to Z of the Royal Arte, the beginning and end of all things. Azoth is the One Thing, which is both the chaotic First Matter at the beginning of the Work and the perfected Stone at its conclusion.

The Philosopher's stone, which begins its creation in the leaden darkness of the alchemical cauldron. From the lowest creature the stone is derived. Hidden in the head of the loathsome toad perhaps?

The Poison Path is here, hidden in alchemical allegory, the entheogenic mystery.

Aleister Crowley called Azoth *'the fluid'*, his disciple Kenneth Grant is more explicit;

> "Azoth; An alchemical term for *the fluid*. The combined essences of the fully polarized power-zones in the human male and female organisms."

In his writings Lévi represents the control of the Azoth through the symbol of a woman with her heel upon the head of a serpent. This is a common Catholic image – the Virgin Mary triumphing over carnal desire – but it is also the image Crowley chose for the dancer on The Universe card of his Thoth Tarot. Lévi describes her as a "white woman," "Maia or Maria," treading both a crescent moon and a black serpent. In *Key of the Mysteries*, "The universal agent...is the infernal serpent of the ancient myths...but if Wisdom, mother of the Elohim, puts her foot upon his head, she outwears all the flames which he belches forth, and pours with full hands upon the earth a vivifying light". In *Transcendental Magic*, Lévi identifies this as an image from the Zohar of a magical serpent who is the son of the sun (as Azoth is the living image of the sun or terrestrial sun) who intends to devour the world, but is subdued when the sea, the daughter of the moon, puts her foot upon his head. Allegorically, this seems to describe the technique of controlling a force by the application of its opposite, but Lévi goes further in *Transcendental Magic*: "She who is intended to crush the serpent's head is intelligence, which ever rises above the stream of blind forces. The Kabalists call her the virgin of the sea, whose dripping feet the infernal dragon crawls forward to lick with his fiery tongues, and they fall asleep in delight,". This doctrine is depicted in an illustration accompanying Pascal Beverly Randolph's "Second of the Great Arcanums" concerning "the Immortalization of the Soul."

And what exactly might Aleister Crowley have to say on this subject? Peculiarly, a wealth of information is to be found in his whimsical novella *The Lost Continent*. In this story, the mysterious Zro is the source of all the power of Atlantis, and the object of all the work of the citizens. In one circumstance, he states "...the Quintessence, said they, or Universal Substance (which some strove to identify with Hyle, others with the Luminiferous Aethyr) is the two-in-one, liquid and solid, the former part being also twofold, fluid and gaseous, and the latter earthy and fiery. The combination of these four phases of Zro accounted for the universe." This twofold nature is reminiscent of Crowley's depiction of Baphomet as lion and serpent, hermaphroditic, or in his Book of Lies, a black two-headed eagle. It is also interesting to consider Crowley's spelling of Baphomet (Bafometh), given as "Father Mithras," in *The Book of Thoth*. Mithras, at least in Crowley's day, was believed to be connected to the fire-worship of the Zoroastrians. Another common etymology of Baphomet gives "Baph Metis," or "Baptism of Wisdom." Since the Creed of the Gnostic Mass mentions "one baptism of wisdom," doubtless Crowley was familiar with this theory. Thus Baphomet is fire and water, father and mother.

In another place in *The Lost Continent*, Crowley writes, "...in its ninth stage, it is not only food and drink, but Universal Medicine, if properly understood. For Zro is also a vision and a voice!" To gain a proper understanding of the exact nature of Zro, one simply needs to look up the word in Hebrew: "seed." Or as Albert Pike (American military hero and Mason) says of the Od or astral light, "Therein is the secret fire, living and philosophical, of which all Hermetic philosophers speak with most mysterious reserve: the Universal Seed, the secret whereof they kept, and which they represented only under the figure of the Caduceus of Hermes". This throws a whole new light on the caduceus in Lévi's depiction of Baphomet. It is well to remember, also, that the final evocation of the lion-serpent in Crowley's Gnostic Mass comes directly after the lance thrusts into the cup.

We are told of all the wondrous virtues of Zro, but also that it has the power to fail and become a deadly poison. Zro is all virtue and also all venom, like Baphomet, god and devil both. If the Azoth is so powerful, yet so deadly, how is one to master it? Pike, drawing from Lévi, is perfectly clear: "The Great Work is, above all things, the creation of man by himself; that is to say, the full and entire conquest which he affects of his faculties and his future. It is, above all, the perfect emancipation of his will, which assures him the universal empire of Azoth, and the domain of magnetism, that is, complete power over the universal magical agent".

This idea of the unification of opposites, male and female, first and last matter, as above so below – this the key to Levi's glyph. Baphomet is the All in the sense that Pan is the All, bisexual, chimerical, twirling the twin caduceus serpents. Our Sabbatic goat morphs animals of land and sea and air together. Human and animal combined and this meaning is of course made explicit by those forearm tattoos, solve and coagula.

Fig 5   Advertising for *Les Mystères de la franc-maçonnerie dévoilés* by Léo Taxil

Satanic orgy shocker!

With this brilliant syncretism accomplished Levi's Baphomet grew appropriately shaggy legs. One Léo Taxil (the pen name of Marie Joseph Gabriel Antoine Jogand-Pagès) was an early adopter of this our horned and hoofed God. His sensational book *Les Mystères de la franc-maçonnerie dévoilés*, provided an exposé of Devil worship in the heart of French Freemasonry. The cover artworks of his book say it all.

Taxil's work was part of an elaborate hoax that included a public (though false) conversion to Roman Catholicism and a four-volume history of Freemasonry, which includes accounts of Masonic Satanism drawn from eyewitness testimony. Taxil collaborated on Devil in the Nineteenth Century, in which his informant Diana Vaughan, allegedly the descendent of the Rosicrucian alchemist Thomas Vaughn, recalls Masonic 'satanic orgies'. During one of these events she claimed that Satan had impregnated her with his huge spined phallus. Taxil had distilled the perfect Satanist conspiracy into a series of racy motifs that would later resurface as the delusions of the American and British Satanic child abuse scares of the late 20th century.

It was hardly surprising that his hoax was so successful. The Church in France was nervous of the real political power that Freemasonry might wield. Taxil was only confirming a prejudice that The Terror had deeply embedded. These secret societies really were dangerous.

As the French clergy lapped up Taxil's stories, the Freemasons protested loudly but that only seemed to confirm their guilt. Finally

Fig 6   Advertising for *Les Mystères de la franc-maçonnerie dévoilés* by Léo Taxil.

in 1897 Taxil called a press conference and announced, to a packed room, that the whole thing was a hoax. Of course not everyone believed him (although the crowd, which included senior clergymen, were very, very angry). Part of the success of Taxil's work was that it resonated with what a large number of people thought (including the Holy See at the time). Namely, that there was a covert conspiracy of Templar-Masonic-Satanists who were intend on creating a one-world Luciferian government. Taxil was the man who gave us the New World Order, but for him it was nothing more than a tabloid journalist's trick to ridicule the Catholic Church.

Now is that the truth? So there is no conspiracy? No hidden agenda? Maybe…

The Baphomet design of Levi, filtered through the salacious writings of Taxil, is a graphic designer's wet-dream. An iconic image capable of innumerable variations. Today re-interpretations of Levi's Baphomet are the standard way in which the Devil is represented.

Go on, close your eyes and imagine The Devil. It's Baphomet isn't it? Levi tells us;

> "We recall once more to that terrible number fifteen, symbolized in the Tarot by a monster throned upon an altar, mitred and horned, having a woman's breast and the generative organs of man – a chimera, a malformed sphinx, a synthesis of deformities. Below this figure we read the frank and simple inscription – THE DEVIL. Yes, we confront here that phantom of all terrors, the dragon of all theogonies, the Anriman of the Persians, the Typhon of the Egyptians, the Python of the Greeks, the old serpent of the Hebrews, the fantastic monster, the nightmare, the Croquemitaine, the gargoyle, the great beast of the Middle Ages, and – worse than all these – the Baphomet of the

THE BOOK OF BAPHOMET 109

Fig 7   Baphomet at a Freemason session from the work of Léo Taxil.

Templars, the bearded idol of the alchemist, the obscene deity of Mendes, the goat of the Sabbath...

...the Grand Masters of the Order of the Templars worshipped Baphomet, and caused it to be worshipped by their initiates; yes there existed in the past, and there may be still in the present, assemblies which are presided over by this figure, seated on a throne and having a flaming torch between the horns. But the adores of this sign do not consider, as do we, that it is a representation of the devil; on the contrary, for them it is the god Pan, the god of our modern schools of Philosophy, the god of the Alexandrian theugic school and of our own mystical Neo-platonists, the god of Lamartine and Victor Cousins, the god of Spinoza and Plato, the god of the primitive Gnostic school; the Christ also of the dissident priesthood."

Fig 8 Goat's head pentagram from *La Clef de la Magie Noire* by Stanislas de Guaita.

Stars in their eyes

Eliphas Levi also provided the template for another of the key images associated with Baphomet (and therefore Satan). Writing in *Transcendental Magic* he discusses the pentagram;

"The Pentagram, which in Gnostic schools is called the Blazing Star, is the sign of intellectual omnipotence and autocracy. It is the Star of the Magi; it is the sign of the Word made flesh; and, according to the direction of its points, this absolute magical symbol represents order or confusion, the Divine Lamb of Ormuz and St. John, or the accursed goat of Mendes. It is initiation or profanation; it is Lucifer or Vesper, the star of morning or evening. It is Mary or Lilith, victory or death, day or night. The Pentagram with two points in the ascendant represents Satan as the goat of the Sabbath; when one point is in the ascendant, it is the sign of the Saviour. By placing it in such a manner that two of its points are in the ascendant and one is below, we may see the horns, ears and beard of the hierarchic Goat of Mendes, when it becomes the sign of infernal evocations."

Not much later, in 1897 French nobleman and occultist Stanislas de Guaita provides us with an illustration of exactly what Levi meant in his *La Clef de la Magie Noire*.

Fig 9   Detail of a stele of King Melishipak I (1186–1172 BC), showing a version of the ancient Mesopotamian eight-pointed star symbol of the goddess Ishtar. Excavated by Jacques de Morgan photograph by Marie-Lan Nguyen.

Within only a few years this potent sign is popping up in all manner of occult texts.

Samael, Lilith, Leviathan – names to conjure with.

By 1961 Maurice Bessy reproduces the inverted pentagram and goat's head in his *Histoire en 1000 Images de la Magie*. Three years later his work is translated into English as *A Pictorial History of Magic and the Supernatural*. The book has a reproduction of this image on its hardback cover (hidden by a tacky dust jacket). The image is rendered in striking white on black, devoid of the Latin letters but retaining the Hebrew. It is this volume that Anton LaVey leaves ostentatiously lying about in the photo shoots to promote The Church of Satan. And so the hypothesised 'sigil of Baphomet' (as LaVay came to refer to it) migrated from the mind of Levi into the popular modern consciousness. Baphomet was Satan, the Sabbatic Goat head, described with the Inverted Pentagram. This was the logo of The Lord of this World and of the antinomian philosophy espoused by Satanists.

The octogram also appears in association with Baphomet, notably in the supposed forms of the idol reproduced by Hammer-Purgstall in *The Guilt of the Templars* (1855). The figure shown is female and perhaps this is one of the connections with the eight-fold star. Sure Baphomet is generally written with eight letters but this eightfold symbolism also turns up in the ancient iconography of the goddess Ishtar/Inanna. Eight is perhaps derived from the astronomical calculations associated with her worship. Remember this lady is Ashtoreth, goddess of lust and sacred prostitution? She rides on a lion.

The Woman astride the Beast.

Goddess

I look up at the God in my arms, brown and green skin, furry thighs between mine; I see him crystal clear, as real as any thing. I close my eyes and I see my self as a bifurcated river flowing around his rock, the rushing torrents of my flesh desperately seeking to encase his shape, grasp his shoulders from beneath, hanging on to his solidity, fucking him from the outside while he fucks me inside. What Goddess am I? I wonder. In my deep trance state I seek amongst the list…

Babalon, passion and fury. Gaia, earth mother, soil plants blood and geological movements. Diana, goddess of the chase, proficient huntswoman. Tara, youthful and wise, spreading enlightenment. Lakshmi, bestowing blessings upon all.

Chaos. I see her so often, the ever present swirl and multi-tudinous input of sensory streams, continually arising, beautiful in the moment and transient as a flower; the knowledge of change and destruction an integral part of her fundamental nature. Chaotic images blossom, colours and shapes signifying all manner of things. A central stem of white prima material twists, growing branches from the ends of which fruit every type of object I have ever seen, alive and manufactured alike. Hyperreal details and a depth of field spanning the entire carousel of the universe.

I speak to my God, answering his words of wanting to fill me, with my words of wanting to flow around him. Each of us sees ourselves as the fluid, the other as solidity; our bodies felt as watery movement from within, seen as earth objects from without. As we express the internalised sensations and desires a third metaphor emerges, of rivers meeting and boundaries dissolving. The identities remain, but the edges blur, we cannot tell where we begin or end.

After the peaks of infinite complexity, when the visions and reflections come hard and fast, we sit face to face, remembering to breathe, hands upon each other's heart chakras. As the gods depart back to their realms, we open our eyes as ordinary people, a man and a woman. We smile.

Baphomet grows from the stones of the earth, through the living, the works of humankind, words colliding to make new thoughts, and from all of this, magick sparks. A singular god, or a goddess, lacks the conversational ability to progress; yet with multiple characters we lose the sense of deity, a community of gods reads like an esoteric soap opera, sagas of wife swapping petty theft and grand design construction.

Yet we need deity; it models a long-term perspective, gives a grand narrative to our daily grind, anthropomorphosises endless space and time. Our deep biological sense of identity means that the sex of a deity affects our responses and relationship with him or her; a neuter spirit feels too distant however so what do we do?

Like those pictures which slide and switch between a hunched over old woman and a poised young lady, Baphomet has attributes indicating both sexes; we see hir primarily as that which we require for any given moment or supplication, while knowing sHe has the wisdom of both (in a Binah experiential kind of way). By seeing both ways, sHe gains the third mind of archetypes, the fractal boundary that dances between dark and light, male and female, dead and living, all clear separations, yet with an edge that recedes the closer we approach.

Replacing our previous main deity, the big beard in the sky that is Jehovah/Allah, with a female version of the same, would never satisfy today's populace, who have grown up internalising the network systems theory of functionality. We disapprove of controlling entities, whether bureaucratic political or religious, believing in bottom up decision-making and values derived from our wider experiential knowledge instead of faith filled books.

In sexual congress we can under certain circumstances, given set and settings to promote this state, approach close to this combined perceptual state of two in another third mind.

Keenly aware of our lover's senses, and wishing to fill them with sensation, we put ourselves in their place; concentrating the mind on giving pleasure, whilst the body receives it, we reach that state of simultaneous observer and experiencer so sort after by the dedicated meditator.

The Tell-Tale Head

But what of Baphomet the head? What of the Templar confessions of the polished idol 'with bright carbuncles for eyes, which shone like the light of heaven'?

Some authors suggest that this skull was the actual object of Templar veneration. An underground head cult, possibly worshipping a relic believed to be the head of John the Baptist. Maybe it was the image of the head of Our Lord on the Turin shroud that may have been part of the Templar treasure. Even more fantastic, perhaps the head was of that of a woman. There are accounts of a reliquary of Templar origin "A great head of gilded silver, most beautiful, and constituting the image of a woman. Inside were two head bones, wrapped in a cloth of white linen, with another red cloth around it." Some writers have even suggested that the head was that of Christ himself. The Gnostic husk left behind while only the pure spirit of the Lord ascended to heaven.

Bearded or not, male or female, naked bone or gilded with metal, head cults have always been pretty popular. Ever since the Upper Palaeolithic period at least. This really is that old time religion.

The original charge sheet drawn up against the Templars in 1308 specifically mentions a head, or skull;

Item, that they said the head could save them.

Item, that [it could] make riches.

Item, that it made the trees flower.

Item, that [it made] the land germinate.

If our mythic death's head is female that could provide another mystic explanation.

Kenneth Grant writes; "That it had a feminine origin is shown by Gerald Massey who writes 'METE was the BAPHOMET or mother of breath'. According to Von Hammer, the formula of faith inscribed on a chalice belonging to the Templars is as follows: "Let METE be exalted who causes all things to bud and blossom, it is our root; it is one and seven; it is octinimous, the eight-fold name."

This head, it would seem, is full of the regenerative influence. A symbol of base fertility, Baphomet is nature, life, and fertility. Here then is a cultural echo of the presumed Celtic head cult. Evidence cited to support the existence of such a cult includes Roman writers such as Livy. In 216 BC a Roman general called Postumius was killed by the Gauls. Livy tells us they;

> "*Stripped his* corpse, severed the head, and bore their prize in triumph to their most sacred temple. There, according to their habit, they cleaned it, decorated the skull with gold and employed *it as a sacred vessel for the pouring of libations for the priests and acolytes of the temple to drink from.*"

Far to the east, one is reminded of the Agora sadhus who gather by the burning ghats, smeared with ash, holding out bowls for alms made from human skulls. These Tantric adepts meditate sitting astride corpses, rave in their datura induced delirium and generally act pretty crazy. Cannibalistic devotees of Shiva. Sitting cross-legged in the forest of funeral pyres, their own skulls shaggy with matted locks. Wild men.

Enter the Horned God

When Egyptologist and folklorist Margaret Murray wrote *The Witch-cult in Western Europe* in 1921 she was riding on the wave of a huge cultural change. This was the re-sexualising of divinity. Crowding around the end of the 19th and beginning of the 20th century are a plethora of books that purported to demonstrate the sexual basis of ancient, and perhaps contemporary, religion.

The 1865 edition of Richard Payne Knights' 1786 essay on Priapus worship was published with an additional essay by antiquarian Thomas Wright. In 1899 American folklorist Charles Leland published *Aradia, or the Gospel of the Witches*. This Castenada-style document was allegedly the religious text of Tuscan witches who venerated Diana as the Queen of the Witches. Diana gives birth to Aradia, the messiah of the disenfranchised peasants, who teaches them witchcraft. Her incestuous father is Diana's brother; Lucifer who (despite the paucity of Biblical information) claims many of the insignia of Baphomet. Those angel wings have become those of the bat. Lucifer puffed with his pride, a flaming light at his head, wild hair and often horns.

Such writings lay the groundwork for the fantastic interpretation of witchcraft that Murray would provide; namely that witches were in fact a Pagan religion that existed concurrently, though covertly, during the Christian period.

As the 19th century tipped over into the 20th the orgies that Léo Taxil had beautifully imagined in his fin de siècle hoax had been given a kind of historical and spiritual legitimacy. In part this was because Freud had opened the Pandora's box of the psyche in his *Interpretation of Dreams*. What Freud had discovered was that sex was the driving force of the mind. Murray wrote that the witchcult was one of open sexuality, secret rebellion against the church and that the Satan of the witches' trials was in fact the joyous horned god. In her work she was elaborating a story that would soon become reality.

By the mid 1970s hundreds of actual naked witches would be dancing round fires, invoking a horned deity of freedom and eroticism. The Horned God had arrived.

Murray's work crystallised a myth about the horned god and the meaning of witchcraft. The power of this myth was sufficient to carry Baphomet into a whole new orbit. Although now discredited in historical circles (and indeed the circles of many modern naked witches) the Murryite hypothesis locked into a powerful poetic truth. Indeed though she was a greatly respected Egyptologist it is just possible that Margaret Murray chose to sacrifice her reputation as a scholar to support the emerging neo-Paganism, a new religion whose time she felt had arrived. The name of Baphomet is infrequent in the emerging neo-pagan cannon but the imagery of Levi's Devil/God Goat of Mendes, becomes a central strand in this part of our story. And that image becomes associated with the classical deity Pan.

In Victorian England Pan was most certainly not dead. Horned deities began populating an imagined English arcadia. They grinned out of the greenwood at those visionary Romantic poets Wordsworth, Keats and Shelly. There are many reasons why a minor league Greek deity like Pan (described by Professor Ronald Hutton as 'the Citron 2CV of gods') became so popular at this time. The 19th century in Britain had seen a huge shift in population distribution as the industrial revolution kicked in. Like J.R.R.Tolkein, longing for his lost Shire, people were fascinated by the lost wilderness of Nature. Whether

Pan is nice or nasty depends on who you read. Arthur Machen terrorises us in his *Great God Pan*, whereas the humble Ratty and Mole get to glimpse this sylvan deity as *The Piper at the Gates of Dawn*.

By 1931 Murray has fleshed out her picture of the Horned God in *The God of the Witches*. Her depiction of the Horned God is enriched by many ancient sources such as the Palaeolithic cave art reported by Henri Breuil from an area of the Trois-Frères, Ariège cave in France know as 'The Sanctuary'. In that underground darkness dances the horned god, emerging into the dawn of the modern period.

When the founding father of modern Witchcraft, Gerald Gardner, published *Witchcraft Today* in 1954 (for which Murray wrote the foreword, simultaneously writing off her career), he could confidently assert the fact that the Templars had been practitioners of the Old Religion. Gardner breathed magical life into Murray's creation. The Horned God became fixed in his cult of Wicca. Gardner even gives a nod to the cult of the head in his book.

> "…In the old days it was said that 'when the god was not present, he was represented by a skull and crossbones ('Death and what lies beyond'. Or 'paradise and regeneration'). Nowadays this is symbolised by the High Priestess, standing with her arms crossed to represent the skull and crossbones…

During this prayer to the High Priestess she opens her arms to the Pentacle position. She then represents the goddess, or regeneration, signifying that the prayer is granted. 'Thus she has been both god and goddess, male and female, death and regeneration, one might say bi-sexual'. Now in Payne Knight's illustrations of Baphomet, said to be the Templar god, he is shown as both male and female or bisexual; sometimes a skull appears, sometimes the moon. Whether there is really and good proof that these are the Templars gods I cannot say. All this may be mere coincidence."

Baphomet does not explicitly figure in *The Book of Shadows*, instead within the witch cult we find our horned god named as Karnayna, Kernunnos, 'The Lord of Animals'. Inanna does not feature explicitly (though her Sister Astarte is named in the ritual poem *The Charge of the Goddess*, and her mythic descent into the underworld is one of the great ritual dramas of the cult). However the fact that she is sometimes imagined as a horned goddess in the ancient world, is absent from Wicca. In Gardner's depiction of the Old Religion it is most emphatically the divine masculine principle that is horned.

Kernunnos is one of those deities who seem to have relations everywhere. In India we find early seals from Mohenjo-daro (the Mound of the Dead) an ancient city of the Indus valley culture. These seals depict what some scholars claim is a horned proto-Shiva. It strongly resembles the figure featured, along with horned serpents and animals that may well be elephants, on the Gundestrup cauldron. On that remarkable example of 1st century BC silverware, found in Denmark, our horned god is either seated in an asana, like Levi's Baphomet, or perhaps dancing like Shiva Nataraja.

Literally named in the proto-Celtic *Cerno-on-os meaning "great horned one", the God of Witches is invoked in the chant witches employ to raise the cone of power at their meetings; the Witches Rune.

Queen of heaven, queen of hell,
Hornéd hunter of the night
Lend your power unto the spell,
And work our will by magick rite!
By all the power of land and sea,
By all the light of moon and sun,
As we will, so mote it be.

Chant the spell and be it done!

Eko, Eko, Azarak
Eko, Eko, Zomulak
Eko, Eko, Cernunnos
Eko, Eko, Aradia!

What is this Wicca really all about? Plenty of ink (including an increasing amount from academic pens) has been spilt in exploring the multi-faceted phenomena of modern witchcraft. As a magick system Wicca works by polarity, simply put it is the exquisite sexual tension in the circle that drives the current of witch energy. The dancing may well raise the Cone of Power but the power rises from the darkness, the skyclad bodies, the kissing of cocks and breasts. This is the fuel that ignites what otherwise might be a series of rather dull quasi-Masonic psychodramas.

Witchcraft is a cult of ecstasy. The immediate apprehension of the divine, as Nature, through gnostic joy. The Book of Shadows is much more a grimoire than a revealed text; it is an adaptable guidebook to a series of ecstatic states accessible through this modern mystery religion. Here devotees worship the Anima Mundi, the World Soul, imagined as a Goddess, and as a horned beast. And like any mystery religion you've got to do it before it makes any sense – direct experience is necessary.

Witchcraft is also the bastard child of that most intriguing and larger-than-life adept, Aleister Crowley. It's time to look at another beast who named himself Baphomet.

The story is that when Theodor Ruess, head honcho of the Ordo Templi Orientis, met Crowley in 1910 he challenged him over his publicly revealing the secret of sexual magick. By writing about Adepts armed with 'mystical roses' and 'magic roods' Ruess claimed that

Crowley had given the game away. Wisely Ruess offered to take Crowley from the cold and into his quasi-Masonic style group. Crowley accepted, took the magical name Baphomet, and began re-designing the Ordo Templi Orientis into the vehicle for his new cult of Thelema.

Following the strand of Baphomet as horned deity Crowley was of course already well versed in all things horny. He'd previously written his inspired *Hymn to Pan*.

All-devourer, all begetter;
Give me the sign of the Open Eye,
And the token erect of thorny thigh,
And the word of madness and mystery,

The OTO became Crowley's organ of choice for promulgating his Word of Thelema. Through Brother Scire (Gerald Gardner, who joined around 1945) Crowley had a channel into the emerging witchcult. The OTO was also allied with the Gnostic Catholic Church and in this way Crowley was very astutely backing several horses at once. The Great Beast's ideas would be coded into the DNA of the neo-Pagan movement, the ceremonial magick tradition (via the OTO) and the renegade Christianity of the Gnostic Catholic Church. Crowley realised that Freemasonry was the perfect vector for his plans since it touches upon so many esoteric styles. He claimed in *The Book of Lies* that Baphomet was the keystone to the symbolism of the Scottish Rite of Freemasonry. Baphomet is thus at the narrative heart of Crowley's magickal work; 'the method of science, the aim of religion'.

The Gnostic Mass, given by Crowley in *Liber XV*, names Baphomet;

> "And I believe in the Serpent and the Lion, Mystery of Mystery, in His name BAPHOMET."

Baphomet for Crowley is the bestial outpouring of the union of Chaos and Babalon. An image he develops further in the depiction he realised, with Freda Harris, in Atu XV, the Devil.

> "This card is attributed to the letter 'Ayin, which means an Eye, and it refers to Capricornus in the Zodiac. In the Dark Ages of Christianity, it was completely misunderstood. Eliphas Levi studied it very deeply because of its connection with ceremonial magic, his favourite subject; and he re-drew it, identifying it with Baphomet, the ass-headed idol of the Knights of the Temple…But at this time archaeological research had not gone very far; the nature of Baphomet was not fully understood… At least he succeeded in identifying the goat portrayed upon the card with Pan."

Crowley identified Baphomet with Shaitan of the Yezidi and Satan of the Jews.

Following the goat shaped symbolism Crowley tell us that the astrological sign associated with Atu XV

> "…Capricornus is rough, harsh, dark, even blind; the impulse to create takes no account of reason, custom, or foresight. It is divinely unscrupulous, sublimely careless of result.
>
> "thou hast no right but to do thy will. Do that, and no other shall say nay. For pure will, unassuaged of purpose, delivered from the lust of result, is every way perfect." AL. I, 42-4.

It is further to be remarked that the trunk of the Tree pierces the heavens; about it is indicated the ring of the body of Nuith. Similarly, the shaft of the Wand goes down indefinitely to the centre of earth.

> "If I lift up my head, I and my Nuit are one. If I droop down mine head, and shoot forth venom, then is rapture of the earth, and I and the earth are one." AL. II, 26. "

As the Great War came to an end the Wizard Amalantrah was asked by Crowley, during an excursion to the astral plane, how Baphomet should be spelt. A sure-fire way, with the application of a little gematria, to discovering the inner nature of any symbol. 'A man like the gods of the mountains' in the vision provided B-a-f-o-m-e-t-h. This variant generates a Hebrew numeration of 729. This number, at the risk of lulling you, gentle reader, to sleep, is 365 (the solar year) plus 364 (the lunar year). It is also the cube of 9. Another leading light in the Wiccan community, Doreen Valiente, likes this and says as much in her 1978 publication *Witchcraft for Tomorrow*. She points out that the Greek numeration of Belçnos (the Ancient British sun God) plus Andatç (the lunar Goddess worshipped by Boadicea) also equals 729. The case, if you're down with gematria, is thus proven.

This sexual magick that so fascinated Crowley was the process by which he created Azoth, that mysterious substance that Levi links to Baphomet. For Crowley Baphomet is both the leaping capricious form of Pan and the androgynous union of opposites. Like Vril and Zro, Azoth is powerful stuff, the literal saviour of the world; Crowley has replaced the messianic Lamb of God with the riotous explosion of the lusty goat.

In the thinly veiled erotic ritual of *The Star Sapphire* Crowley tells us that:

> "In this the Signs shall be those of Set Triumphant and of Baphomet. Also shall Set appear in the Circle. Let him drink of the Sacrament and let him communicate the same."

In this Holy Book Crowley chooses the term Ararita rather than Azoth although the meaning is much the same, it is a Notariqon (or acronym) of the Hebrew phrase "One [is] his Beginning; One [is] his Individuality; his Permutation [is] One."

In *Book Four* Crowley clearly links Baphomet, as the horned beast, to that other creature that has been writhing around the Templars, the snake.

"This serpent, SATAN, is not the enemy of

Man, but He who made Gods of our race, knowing Good and Evil; He bade "Know thyself!" and taught Initiation. He is

"the Devil" of the Book of Thoth, and His emblem is

BAPHOMET, the Androgyne who is the hieroglyph of arcane

perfection. The number of His Atu is XV, which is Yod He,

the Monogram of the Eternal, the Father one with the Mother,

the Virgin Seed one with all-containing Space. He is

therefore Life, and Love. But moreover his letter is Ayin,

the Eye; he is Light, and his Zodiacal image is Capricornus,

that leaping goat whose attribute is Liberty."

This description reminds one of those horned serpents held by the horned deity on the Gundestrup cauldron, the serpentine caduceus of Levi's Goat of Mendes and that mysterious lady dancing with the snake.

To bring Baphomet up to date we need to explore the associations of those signs; so we ask of the serpent wrangling woman (as Alan Moore asks in his ritual poem *Snakes & Ladders)* 'who's that girl?'

Not with a Bang

It all started with alchemy. The peacock feathers in my mother's bedroom, so exotic to an untravelled English child of the 70s; How could a bird have grown these fabulous objects? Such colours, such patterns, from the pores of the skin? Like my hair grew?

I had a nightmare. Lying in a ditch outside my house, I had leaves growing from my follicles. The big, sweet chestnut kind of leaves, with a long stalk with an attachment point at its base, thick like the base of a hair when you pull one out. I lived in that dream the agony of a leaf falling from my body.

My father drove up to the Hall where I would later hear the lecture about alchemy, long ago. He was delivering oil to the house. There were peacocks in the grounds, too tempting, he chased and trod on their tails, got a handful of feathers to take home to his wife, my mother. Before I was born.

As I write this, I feel so tired. The weariness weighs on me, every hour of the last 4.5 billion years presses against my brain, with images and sounds, sensations and thoughts, plans and dreams, struggling to emerge into awareness simultaneously. And beyond; the legacy of my starry past, homeopathic memories of space dust and white dwarves, right back to the beginning before hours had been invented.

I carry all this with me now. Until this body, I had no idea of the burden of responsibilities I bear. Forgot, with each new birth; unaware of anything more than the fleeting moment of one life at a time.

Today I fall out of bed, stare at the TV set, rather than engage for one second longer with the world that I recognise now as merely part of myself. All is one, therefore experiencing any bit of it makes as much sense as any other bit. All one box in the end.

My muscles ache, my head pounds, throbbing with the pain of all those injuries and deaths, all the information passing into me from every moment of the past, leaving no room for the future.

Food tastes bland and unsatisfying; no emotion touches me these days. All déjà vu.

I wait for death to arrive, hoping that next time round I will avoid the books, the video screens full of stories, and instead live once again in a world of leaves and dirt without mediation.

I hurt, with the agony of having tried, I weep, at the awful realisation that I have now succeeded in my ambition, to understand just what the world has done and how it arrived in the here and now.

Because I cannot see how it will ever end. The suffering, the separation, the loss of painstakingly accumulated knowledge; surely it would make better sense to live in ignorance, and exist as a bottom feeder of the human species, consuming hedonistically without care? We can invent machines to run things for us sensibly, then no-one need ever have to deal with the guilt of all those actions of destruction, wanton cruelty, blood pouring through the cobbled streets of civilised revolutions, animals ripped apart for their warm flesh, land ploughed into submission, destroying the lives of countless billions of lifeforms, screaming in silence...

And I only carry the responsibility of my species. Were I to extend my sorrow to the millions of other species, red in tooth and claw, how much worse it would become; the mystics of my time tell me to reach out and join my consciousness to theirs, those creeping multitudes which savage each other, dying of cold, heat, exhaustion, predation, injury without medicine to ease the exit from life's vicious traps. Sheer madness!

What possible experiences could ever hope to begin to compensate for all this absolute misery? Once I viewed sunsets, and sighed, thinking how this beauty was worth a thousand blows to happiness. Now I am old, I think again.

So why keep living? Why not give up and call it a day?

Second thoughts. Perhaps, maybe, there will come an ultimate experience that will convince me of the Why and the Wherefore of it all.

I keep searching.

I drag myself away from the familiar, out into the world of unknowns, all the variations on that theme, recombining old happenings in new ways, trying to create the harmonic resonance of a new note. The curse of the creative, each time I succeed I doom that attempt to failure, for the new is old having been seen.

This too shall pass.

I should resign myself to life on the sofa, passively absorb the screenshots into my retinas, lie back and think of England. Especially as a female body, receptive, quiescent.

Often I wish my mind fitted the stereotype, would leave the thinking to others cleverer and wiser than myself. Except of course they are part of me, from a universal consciousness perspective... how does that work? No man is an island, so why do I get drawn into philosophical and political debates, when my opinion has no effect on the world? Why do I persist in analysing, finding alternatives, telling my fellow commoners my opinions and remedies? How do we change things?

Bluster, rhetoric, empty gestures signifying nothing.

Science doesn't change the way things are. Neither does what passes for Art these days. Religion died a long slow death many centuries ago, the zombie priests repeating meaningless litanies to their flocks. Does Magick hold the answer? I've lived magick deeply and thoroughly, for my whole adult life, and most of my childhood too. It weaves into every breathe I take, every word I speak, each blink of my eyes. Can it transmogrify the world anew with the passage of time, hidden between the 13Hz (give or take 9Hz...) refresh rate of working memory, the tiny slit through which we view existence and construct that problematic theoretical construct, consciousness? Taken as a proportion of overall life, the infinitesimal frame of input we get around 13 times each second means we remain mostly unaware of what happens around us. The Doors of Perception flash open like the shutter on a projector, and who knows what happens in the vast unperceived darkness meantime?

They tell me the past only exists as potential possibilities, as does the future. So can I, can we, forget that which we dislike? Or regret? Not while reminders continue. However much attention I withdraw, the broken part of my head recurs on a daily basis, poking me into acceptance of past times' reality, now. I tell you, next time I have a brain injury, I won't tell anyone, and then it'll be able to disappear without a trace.

If I remember to forget, that is.

Which ultimately proves as impossible as winning The Game; damn I've lost again! You know the game, the kids all play it; the game is to forget the game. If you remember that, you lose.

I would like to win the game of history, and forget all I know, start again from today. Well, maybe keep a few instruction books and gadgets. Ah but, that's where it all falls apart you see. Keep one thing and the trail leads back to wars and famines, exploration and exploitation.

Can we win the game, leave those old quarrels, the weariness and guilt, the feeling of responsibility? Whilst carrying the fruits of our ancestors' labour into the brave new world of tomorrow?

Beyond paradox the neither-neither realm awaits us. Dare we load up an Ark with the good, wash away the bad, look around and claim the world starts today? Not likely...

Serpent Dance

Frieda Harris and Aleister Crowley created in their Thoth tarot a gorgeous image of a woman dancing with a serpent. Atu XXI The Universe is just that, the glyph of the Whole. The backdrop to our dancing figures is;

> "…the skeleton plan of the building of the house of Matter. It shews the ninety-two known chemical elements, arranged according to their rank in the hierarchy."

The house of Matter, the Temple of Solomon.

For Crowley there could be no more magickal a sign of the universe than the periodic table, but what is crucial here is the next part of Crowley's commentary on the card:

> "All these symbols swim and dance in a complex but continuous ambience of loops and whorls. The general colour of the traditional card is subfusc; it represents the confusion and darkness of the material world. But the New Aeon has brought fullness of Light; in the Minutum Mundum, Earth is no longer black, or of mixed colours, but is pure bright green. Similarly, the indigo of Saturn is derived from the blue velvet of the midnight sky, and the maiden of the dance represents the issue from this, yet through this, to the Eternal. This card is to-day as bright and glowing as any in the Pack."

For the magician and writer Alan Moore (who memorably staged a performance of his *Snakes and Ladders* which included a woman dancing with a python to act out the part of Atu XXI) the identity of these figures is clear:

> "Look closer still, and she is hardly there at all, pale and ethereal, translucent, made from moonlight. She is life's sole partner in this waltz of Being, yet she is imaginary, more than this, she is imagination, the most beautiful and splendid partner we could ever need; could ever hope for.
>
> Naked save for the moonshine, save the borrowed finery of Isis and Selene, she inspired our dance to new and unfamiliar steps, gives us the come-on. Sexier than anything imagination moves our feet upon the rungs of the genetic ladder, leads us from insensate slime and into consciousness. Dances us up from dumb, cold mud into the blazing heavens."

Our Lady is the World Soul, the consciousness, more properly the imagination; that limitless space that emerges from the finite resources of the universe. Plato digs this saying "Therefore, we may consequently state that: this world is indeed a living being endowed with a soul and intelligence ... a single visible living entity containing all other living entities, which by their nature are all related." She appears in the hermetic magickal tradition and in the pantheist philosophy of Spinoza.

Moore is echoing Levi's interpretation of this symbol that he described in Transcendental Magic.

> "The sovereign will is represented in our symbols by the Woman who crushes the serpent's head...let us affirm without evasion that the Great Magical Agent – the double

current of light, the living and astral fire of the earth – was represented by the serpent with the head of an ox, goat or dog, in ancient theogonies. It is the dual serpent of the caduceus, the old serpent of Genesis, but also the brazen serpent of Moses, twined about the Tau, that is the generating lingam. It is, moreover, the Goat of the Sabbath and the Baphomet of the Templars; it is the Hyle of the Gnostics; it is the double tail of the serpent that forms the legs of the solar cock of Abraxas".

Levi scatters symbols like a psychotic Typhonian, forges link upon mythic link.

Woman is awareness, limitless mind that rises from the serpentine shape. In modern times we might naturally imagine this as our DNA, that fantastical molecule that drives our form. The serpent takes on a different head, becomes horned, lion headed or otherwise transmuted into a symbol of unity: Baphomet.

The magickal formula is deceptively simple.

When Woman dances with the serpent, Baphomet arises.

When imagination apprehends the material world that generates it then we are no longer the Fallen. Instead we rise and, seeing the world as it truly is, the world itself becomes conscious.

Science is a manifestation of that gnostic approach whereby we behold naked reality. Science is an outpouring of that secret wisdom which was cherished by occult societies down the centuries. The adepts of Atlantis are imagined as one of those groups, as are the Templars. Our Woman dancing is the Periodic Table, the conscious apprehension of the universe by itself.

The scene has been set. The candles and incense have been lit. Time for the curious child science to embrace its parent, magick, and for a new cultus to emerge that places Baphomet at its heart; Chaos Magick.

Embrace the Chaos

Peter J. Carroll, one of the founding figures of the chaos magickal approach, says of Baphomet:

"Baphomet is the psychic field generated by the totality of living beings on this planet. Since the Shamanic aeon, it has been variously represented as Pan, Pangenitor, Panphage, All-Begetter, All-Destroyer, as Shiva-Kali – creative phallus and abominable mother and destroyer – as Abraxas – polymorphic god who is both good and evil – as the animal headed Devil of sex and death, as the evil Archon set over this world, as Ishtar or Astaroth – goddess of love and war – as the Anima Mundi or World Soul, or simply as '"Goddess." Other representations include the Eagle, or Baron Samedi, or Thanateros, or Cernunnos – the horned god of the Celts."

Carroll favours the conjecture that our god's name comes from the Greek Baph-Metis, Union with wisdom. The clear identification of Baphomet with Thanateros explains why this deity is central to the culture of the magickal group Carroll founded – The Magical Pact of the Illuminates of Thanateros, the IOT. The key ritual in the IOT cannon that invokes Baphomet is the Mass of Chaos B (i.e. Baphomet). In this ritual Carroll defines how, through each successive aeon, Baphomet is perceived. In his formulation of the Mass he has our horned deity declare:

IN THE FIRST AEON, I WAS THE GREAT SPIRIT

IN THE SECOND AEON, MEN KNEW ME AS THE HORNED GOD, PANGENITOR PANPHAGE

IN THE THIRD AEON, I WAS THE DARK ONE THE DEVIL

IN THE FOURTH AEON, MEN KNOW ME NOT, FOR I AM THE HIDDEN ONE

IN THIS NEW AEON, I APPEAR BEFORE YOU AS BAPHOMET THE GOD BEFORE ALL GODS WHO SHALL ENDURE TO THE END OF THE EARTH

Critics of chaos magick occasionally misunderstand its orientation around the 'results magick' that practitioners of this style commonly avow. However a rite such as the Mass of Chaos B certainly indicates a wider purpose for magick than simply a trick that has been characterised as wanking over a sigil on a post-it note to ensure that one's benefit cheque arrives promptly. Instead Baphomet points the way to the broader application and meaning of the chaos approach. In personal terms this means that process of Illumination or Enlightenment, and on a social level, the desire of the mage to assist in the birth of the new aeon.

Ok so we're getting all messianic now! Hardly surprising in members of a secret society that identifies itself with the Illuminati! Sure, let's Immanentize the Eschaton!

The (re)birth of Baphomet into the chaos approach isn't easy. Pete Carroll recalls one incident:

> "There was also a demented event at Trinity Hall in Bristol at a rock concert at which Dave Lee was present. It was ill-

conceived and badly executed and the organisation fell down completely, there was some fighting...

Go on Pete, tell us the story!

"This shambolic event in the early eighties arose because of contacts between members of my Bristol Temple and the musician Mark Stewart. It had been apparently agreed that we would meet before the gig for a rehearsal where we would improvise something to go with some of his music for a midwinter rite on stage at midnight on the solstice. In the event we turned up about 8pm but neither Mark nor any of the props or any rehearsal opportunity were available. We sat around for hours and the venue filled up with punky and anarchistic and alternative types. Finally we got word that we should just go on stage and do our stuff. Well we hadn't actually got anything planned and one of the group was having a relationship breakdown on the spot and had gotten pretty drunk whilst waiting. I suggested that we just forget the whole thing but members were keen to do something, some having travelled a long way, and all having waited all evening. My last words to them were, well I'll start it, you finish it."

They all robed and masked up and lit their flaming torches. I emerged from behind a speaker bank and welcomed the solstice as the day of greatest darkness and then launched into a growling rendition of the Baphomet invocation, then I retreated behind the speaker bank and let them get on with it. They trooped onto stage in the robes and masks with the flaming torches and suddenly someone we vaguely knew on the fringes of the scene leaps up in front of the stage and starts to deliver the Lesser Banishing Ritual with gusto. Then the crazily drunk member of our group goes forward to the edge of the stage and attempts to set fire to the guy using his flaming torch. The guy grabs it just below the flaming edge and hurls it away, so the crazed guy takes a few paces back and then hurls himself off the stage at the banisher. Then the bouncers pile in and there is some disorder, torches get dropped amongst the wiring littering the stage, the audience seems to be getting a bit wild. I'm not sure exactly what happens next, people are running around shouting, I grab a mike and announce that the Manifestation of Chaos is at an end. Well, maybe it is, but the disorder continues. I retrieve my unused robes from backstage and prepare to leave. I bump into Mark who says something like, hell, I've got to go on now and deal with this maddened audience. It seems that the bouncers manage to restrain the crazy guy and eject him but shortly afterwards he crashes back in through the front door and runs with a maddened scream down towards the stage, the bouncers tackle him and rough him up a bit apparently, but I don't see this. I didn't stay for the Mark Stewart gig, it was by then very late.

Anyway, we catch up with the crazed guy the next day, he has plenty of bruises but nothing serious, and he later goes on to form a notable alternative social-political protest organization."

For many years, The Mass of Chaos B was often attended by incidents of spilled wine and chaotic rage. As the IOT matured, the Mass altered slightly; an atmosphere of harmonious diversity provided Baphomet with a less fearful welcome, and joyous celebration became the general default setting. Yet, Baphomet provokes awe within us, and still expresses rage against the worst extremes of mass scale uncaring and willfull destruction of lives. We ask hir for blessings upon and power to those who embody through their actions the evolutionary path of best ecological results; diversity, efficiency, resilience, and above all the opening of possibilities to the many rather than the few.

Global Baphometic gnosis… for aeons the human species lived as animals, dancing, singing, building nests and homes for themselves, making tools, laughing and playing and fighting. We knew ourselves

Fig 10   Baphomet by Frater Tadhg.

as part of the flow of everything that lived around us. We ate, we were eaten, plants and animals metamorphosing one into another. Obviously, everything alive was one substance, a clay from which forms sprang, lived, then fell back into the dark embrace of Earth.

Today then. We've heard the historical story and lineage of this deity Baphomet, and how the IOT identified it with the Great Spirit. But what of the rest of the planet? As a genuine real life GodDess, Baphomet should be raising hir profile everywhere we look.

Certainly the name Baphomet itself continues to be a major symbol for the conspiracy theories of modern times. Working away in the realm of half-truth, spinning the mythic tapestry of the modern age.

In his book *The Essene Odyssey*, published a few years before his death Dr. Hugh J. Schonfield (who worked on the Dead Sea Scrolls) suggests that the word 'Baphomet' was created with knowledge of the Atbash substitution cipher. This code substitutes the first letter of the Hebrew alphabet for the last, the second for the second last, and so on. "Baphomet" rendered in Hebrew and transformed using Atbash can be interpreted as the Greek word 'Sophia', or wisdom. This theory is an important part of the plot of Dan Brown's 2003 conspiracy detective story The Da Vinci Code. But outside of such shadowy speculation where can we see the mark of the Baphomet Beast in wider culture, what are the signs by which we shall know it?

The Will to Live

The emergence of Baphomet is emblematic of a certain, evolving awareness. Part of this what we might call 'ecological perception'. There are many ways of describing this way of apprehending the universe. Take for example that fact that humans have been described as 'mobile habitats'. Each one of us is in fact a legion of beings or selves. There are thousands of times more bacteria in your guts than there are cells in what you might normally think of as your body. Frequently we describe ourselves as 'beings', as though we were static whereas we are actually a network, a flow, a colony. This holds true (unsurprisingly) at both physical and mental levels. For instance those of us who are numerate use (at least) two distinct systems in our brains to manipulate numbers. Even our apparently unitary sense of self is more like a conspiracy or network than a discrete being.

These neurological facts also point us towards a fantastic possibility. Namely that latent in our bodies, vast unrealised potentials may be hidden. Imagine if one day we discovered a process that joined up two apparently discrete modules in the mind into a new and phenomenally powerful meta-process. This has already happened many, many times; the development of written language is one such instance. We know that these developments, these quantum leaps, can happen fast, sweeping like a virus (or 'meme') through a population. As we seek to join up more things, whether through simple technologies (such as exploring the biological feedback systems connecting sound, emotional state, posture and so forth) or through complex inventions (biofeedback systems, fMRI scanning, global information technologies) there are increased chances of these new abilities emerging.

Of course these new abilities, when they emerge, invariably do so at the limits of experience and in the liminal spaces of the noosphere. In academia it is those transdisciplinary areas that are the richest intellectual ecotones. That's why so many scientists and magicians are working in those fields; there are rich pickings there. Of course this isn't to suggest these discoveries will lead to utopia (though it might not be a bad thing to act 'as if' that were the case). The invention of writing created as many problems as it solved. Not for nothing did King Thamus look askance at Thoth's pharmakon when he came up with the idea of hieroglyphics.

Once we have recognised that we are a merging, transient and yet pervasively permanent colony entity, this cannot fail to affect our magick. Since we are not only 'these bodies' but also 'these systems', naïve forms of Satanism that glory in the self as an adamantine monolith are easily called into question. Instead it makes more sense to seek to generate, through our spells of every kind, a rich, flexible and strong reality. Instead of yelling at our sigils to bring us money, we caress them that they may yield gold.

In the tiny space within the noosphere, on the western spiral arm of the physical galaxy, embedded in the esoteric tactic we call 'chaos magick', Baphomet reminds us of the aeonic role of that magical style. We conjure for a sustainable world, for the application of innovations that will allow our species to prosper. We invoke demons to oppose those who work for short-term profits, and angels to support those who are implementing long-term visions that add value to our planet. Baphomet is first and foremost the deity of the life force of earth. Humanity is waking up to our role and responsibility in terms of that life force. In the twinkling of a geological eye we have made huge impacts on the planet and excelled in a dizzying propagation of technology. We have so deeply influenced the earth that the geological era in which we live is known as the Anthropocene. We have generated a vast number of meta-modules of awareness, many machines and skills. If we are that life force becoming self-aware then our awareness first sees that until now most of us were sleeping. Worse, on awakening we discover that we've been sleep walking, are injured, and that we've made one hell of a mess in the temple. We awake only to discover that we're massively changed the climate, that our current culture is poised on the brink of disaster. We've emerged from the deep sleep of the last 10,000 years and woken to the nightmare of resource depletion, gargantuan weapons, huge social inequality and immanent ecological meltdown. The next stage is to wake fully. To realise Baphomet in all hir forms, to arise from the trance.

Once upon a time one Sister undertook the trance of Baphomet using a powerful psychoactive sacrament. She felt herself dying, and the horror that could accompany that sensation. The violent, terrifying rubbing out of the self. But as she came out of the trance she could hear singing. Each voice bringing her back to life. She described that she knew how all those other voices had, and would have, the experience of dying. And yet even though death was embedded in each one, still the voices sang. As new voices emerged they would in turn take up the song. And this was the joy, the ecstasy of the life force. The voices were singing the name of that force: Baphomet.

But Baphomet the word and name is just a (satanic) indicator. What we might call the 'Baphometic Process', is in fact active on many fronts.

In the field of religion we see the undermining of scriptural doctrines and in many places a revitalisation of a magickal worldview. The shamans are returning to Siberia. We are seeing many syncretic cults that emphasise direct experience of gnosis and not reliance on divine literature. Jesus has returned as the Banisteriopsis vine to members of the Santo Daime Church and encourages his worshippers to say 'give me' when the ayahuasca is passed round. This is not mere Romanticism for an archaic tribal idyll. The shamans of the steppe use credit cards and chi gong is studied with rigorous scientific method in China. The sceptics of paranormal effects can now be found analysing remote viewing data (if only as social phenomena). This cross fertilisation of ideas, this process of looking to direct experience to provide the answers, the desire to develop or perhaps re-kindle a holistic perspective, is everywhere.

Outpourings of the Baphometic processes will probably include huge developments in technologies to directly link the mind with the wider world. Augmented bodies, mentally controlled computers, remotely accessible archives, devices that boost our psychic powers, chemicals that permit us to explore our own neurology – these and more will arise. Critically we also need; ways of producing food that don't deplete the biosphere, successful methods of resolving conflicts before they escalate to global proportions, strategies for curbing population. A viable method of interstellar travel would be handy too.

The Death of Baphomet

As you are reading this you are dying. The little knot of energy in the universe that constitutes you is fast winding down. Watched from the perspective of evolutionary time your own little life is a tiny fluttering of biology. Watched through the eyes of geological time we hardly register at all. Compared to the titanic entropic droop of a universe stumbling towards its heat death (assuming the Standard Model of cosmology, for the moment, to be true) we are as nothing. Yet we certainly feel ourselves to be something. On the immediate scale of humanity our lives, and therefore our deaths, loom large. No culture fails to speak of death. No religion fails to have sometimes fairly detailed instructions about what death means, how it should be prepared for and, critically, what comes after death.

I posed the question 'so what do you think happens when you die' to a number of my magickal colleagues recently and was intrigued by their broad agreement about what happens in the processes of death and dying. This section is inspired by those conversations.

Let us return to the utter unimportance of our own deaths, at least in terms of the Big Picture of the universe. Unless a bold new physics emerges that tells us a new story (and that of course is by no means impossible) we can assume that our own perceptions, our lives and indeed life as a whole, emerge in a relatively brief window of opportunity. Sandwiched between the big bang and the long cold echo that will follow, as all energy becomes evenly distributed across the universe, we exist. Those tiny quantum fluctuations in the first few moments, when space and time were new, have given rise to little islands of possibility. We can detect these in the uneven appearance of the cosmic background radiation (CBR) photographed by our spacecraft. The fact that the very earliest observable signature of the early universe holds such inconstancies means that, rather than being spread out in dull uniformity, denser zones of nascent reality formed. Dust clouds expanded, stars came on, planets aggregated and fell into stable orbits. On at least one of these worlds the complex chemical interaction we call life begins. From a rabble of tiny chaotic butterflies fluttering in the primal Kia, we arise.

This mathematical oddity, this outpouring of increasing complexity in a cosmos that is otherwise running out of steam, can be imagined as Baphomet. The apparently anti-entropic emergence of the ten-thousand things. But if Baphomet is, in one sense, the life-force then that force is both framed within death (the Big Bang and Big Crunch) and peppered with death throughout. Indeed so pervasive is death that biology rides on its back. The teeth that bite, the claws that catch; single celled organisms absorb their neighbours, mycelium the size of cities creep beneath the surface of the soil, spiralling vultures descend the thermals and settle to feed in the towers of silence.

The first point that a number of magicians will make is simply this; given the grand scheme of things why should the death of a human be any more significant (in cosmic terms) than the death of a house fly? Many religions of course claim otherwise. They claim that humans are special, that they are imbued with souls, spirits and all kinds of complex post-mortem shenanigans happen when we shuffle off this mortal coil. But why should this be the case? Does the death of a dolphin, a dog or *Drosophila melanogaster* matter more or less to the universe than that of a human? This of course isn't to say that humans as a species can't do some quite remarkable things, but dying really isn't an unusual behaviour.

Death is welded into the bald fact of our biology. Though there are a very few multi-cellular species (notably *Turritopsis nutricula,* the potentially immortal jellyfish) which can cheat, or at least (in principle), stave off death for considerable periods, as far as we are aware everything alive must die. In the case of humanity it is our understandable fear of death that feeds our desire for life-extension strategies, after-life realities and cryogenic suspension. But it is also the impermanence of life that inspires other aspects of our spiritually. Many forms of Buddhism and Hinduism, with their desire to go beyond the narrow confines of self, embrace death. Christianity is the classic cult of death, growing from the same sandy soil in which the pharaohs were buried, its afterlife promised to the faithful by the bloody sacrifice of God in human form. In praise of this eternal post-mortem paradise great cathedrals are built.

Do magicians hanker after an after-life? Well not those I spoke to. The idea of any 'final state' seems rather silly in terms of the magical world-view. Everything is process, everything is cycle, everything changes, nothing is static. The molecules that constitute our bodies are recycled. Why should it be that, for no obviously reason, an ape that walks upright on a tiny planet, gets to attain some endless non-corporeal state (with the same form of consciousness) as when they lived, once dead? The whole premise seems as preposterous to most occultists as resurrection in the body seems to those who refuse to believe in the literal transubstantiation of the Mass.

Yet this wide-angle view does not seek to trivialise the embodied experience of death for the individual, its obvious cultural significance, or indeed to reduce conscious awareness to some inconsequential epiphenomena of our chemistry. This is because many magicians take the view that the universe is imbued or perhaps even created by a panpsyche, a world soul. Consciousness is implicit in all aspects of the universe. In a simple sense this is the observer effect noted in physics, that observation structures the observed. Consciousness does not merely arise out of the physical structure of the cosmos; it is a fundamental quality of reality, much as space and time are. Indeed many occultists take the view that consciousness is the container of reality. Personally I suspect this view is amenable to scientific enquiry and that it is by understanding the inconsistencies in reality that the CBR alerts us to that we might come to know more. The stochastic, 'random' nature of reality (which gives rise to fractal complexity) is probably the feature of the universe out of which a panpsychic physics and mathematics might develop.

So when we die our consciousness does not, in the panpsychic sense, end. If consciousness is an intrinsic property of the universe, ubiquitous as gravity (indeed it may be *the* underlying fabric of reality) can it really be said to die? Perhaps the 'I', as Spare put it, is 'Atmospheric'. This notion of the panpsychic universe may also explain a human-scale observation of Carl Jung and his student Marie-Louise von Franz, explored in her work *On Dreams & Death*. Namely that the unconscious mind does not behave as though it is going to end. Although it may send signals to the consciousness (in the forms of dreams and synchronicities) that the bodily life is coming to an end, it does not indicate that it in itself, nor its expression as archetypal forces, will end with death.

But what can we say about the personal experience of dying? The natural position of the magician, as you might expect, is that of radical uncertainty. We simply don't know the details of how it feels to die, what if anything happens to awareness after death, and occultists tend to fully acknowledge the contingency of their beliefs. There views are informed by both ancient soul-lore (such as the complex views of post-mortem experience described by Germanic or Egyptian myth) and contemporary ethnographic and scientific exploration. We certainly know that in near death experiences (NDEs) there are narrative elements that are common to many accounts. This isn't any more remarkable than the discovery of form-constants in the entoptic images produced by hallucinogenic drugs or other trance practices. We have a common biology, and while this may be interpreted in the light of different cultural values (I see the horned god/dess Baphomet, you see the Devil), what happens in a NDE is broadly similar across cultures.

A wide variety of researchers have looked into the NDE. Ornella Corazza provides a good summary of current research in her book *Near-Death Experiences: Exploring the Mind-body Connection*. NDE commonly includes elements such as an imagined journey. Corazza compares research into NDEs from western cultures with studies conducted in Japanese, Indian, Chinese & Melanesian cultures. The form of the journey seems to be culturally dependent but whether it is imagined as a road through the mountains, a ride down a river or, as is most common in the west (and in the Tibetan Book of the Dead), travelling through a tunnel towards a bright light, some form of apparent movement happens. These narratives are not rare events; in fact NDEs happen in around 45% of cases of people who have a brush with death (this figure is over 80% in children). So whatever is going on subjectively is a consistent effect, though clothed in the iconography that makes sense to the individual.

Experiences of meeting entities are common. These may be ancestors, supernatural or mythic beings. Again we see, unsurprisingly, what we expect to see. Extrasensory perception and out of body experiences (such as seeing ones body on the operating table, as though from above) are also cross-cultural. A sense of peace and oneness with the universe is common. Less frequent, but also reported, is abject terror. In many NDEs there is a point at which the individual is sent back. They may be told that they must return to their body by a mythical being or simply know that they cannot (yet) go on. For a small number there is the experience of a life review, as memories long lost from conscious recall re-emerge. For many there is the experience of entering, or sometimes seeing in the distance, a beautiful landscape.

Various methods can be used to simulate the NDE. To the magician these are great allies since they would seem to literally allow us to practise our death. Although by no means identical when scrutinised phenomenologically, these experiences provide us with the flavour of what it is like to die. Experiences of electro-stimulation of the temporal lobe, prolonged isolation, Dimethyltryptamine (DMT), nitrous oxide and ketamine all contain NDE-like elements. Corazza's research includes recording people's visions in the ketamine state and looking at these in relation to NDE accounts. There are certainly differences but also significant similarities. This is hardly surprising as Karl Jansen in his ketamine research suggests that the endogenous chemistry of the dying brain stimulates and suppresses neural systems closely associated with those which are affected by ketamine.

Ketamine is also increasingly used in pain management during palliative care in the west and therefore familiarity with the state may be of even more important to the magician. It could well be that this drug will be the last exogenous experience one has before death begins. Knowing the psychic territory from which one might enter the beyond would make sense in terms of being able to let go into death successfully. 'Letting go' is the critical ability for navigating psychedelic drugs, especially at high dose. It would also make sense to deploy this approach when we die. Since most pain is not pain in itself, but is instead generated by our anxiety about our pain, to make death less painful we need to relax. It may be romantic to rage against the dying of the light but when your number's up it will make no difference. Better to focus one's intention on opening fully to the experience. Once you've taken a hit of a powerful psychoactive such as DMT there is no going back. Attempting to hold on to sober reality will only create cramping, collapsing, cruelly twisted visions. Perhaps if we close up at death it is then that ghosts are spawned? Maybe it is also in this way that cases of apparent reincarnation occur. Tragic deaths seem to produce both. In these instances could it be that somehow elements of non-localised consciousness become locked into reality? Either embedded in stone, as haunted houses, or translated into newly forming brain tissue as memories of a previous life. Certainly there are little boys who awake crying; feeling the flames melting their skin and pilot's jacket as a World War II bomber comes crashing down. These cases are ubiquitous and not only to be found in cultures that believe in reincarnation. I asked my magician friends about this. One said 'yes that has a reality'. But this is no simple transcendentalist model where we are therefore seeking to be liberated from that pesky Samsara wheel. Rather this reincarnation is just another aspect of the process of death-consciousness-life. It represents simply one of the many outpouring of our vast, mysterious universe. And while cases such as those documented by psychiatrist Ian Stevenson in his *Twenty Cases Suggestive of Reincarnation* do occur, they do not always lead us back to a world of suffering or seem to be connected by traumatic death. Sometimes reincarnated children are re-born into the same family and surrounded by the love they had once before. Sometimes they turn out to be the new Dalai Lama.

One conjecture about death is that of the eternal moment (see *Now That's What I Call Chaos Magick*). How might such an eternal moment occur in the brain and mind?

We know that the distortion of time is common to many trance states, it certainly occurs with many psychoactive drugs and also perhaps with dying.

One model of psychoactive action proposes that these drugs alter the usual 'refresh rate' of the perceptual systems in the brain. This leads to trails of light, like time-lapse ghost images, emerging from our waving hands as we dance. The perceptual grids that mark the edge detecting elements of our visual system pile up upon each other. This leads to the complex patterns and morphing visuals that accompany many psychedelic states. Inside our minds time is stretched out; thirty minutes may seem like many hours, and an hour like an eternity. Eventually at the high point of a psychedelic trip this pilling up of perceptual data (from both the senses and inner awareness) feedbacks on itself generating an experience in which time stops and everything in awareness becomes simultaneously connected to everything else. Where once there were fractal patterns created by the mathematical interpenetration and recursive layering of the inputs into consciousness, instead white noise and often the 'white light' appears. We hang for a moment, outside the circles of time, in a formless realm. This is the ineffable, timeless peak of the trip.

The chemistry of death contains many processes that could produce such visions. Death of course means that all the cells begin to break down and the resultant chemical soup contains a wide variety of interactions, which we are, as yet, unable to model very satisfactorily. One thing we do know is that during hypoxia, ischaemia, hypoglycaemia, temporal lobe epilepsy and other NDE inducing events, the neurotransmitter glutamate comes rushing out. This glutamate flooding stimulates the N-methyl-D-aspartate, (NMDA) receptors in the brain, overactivating NMDA receptors resulting in neuro ('excito') toxicity. This process is very similar to the blockade of NDMA created by ketamine. NDMA has a critical role in synaptic plasticity and memory. Subjectively we may experience this chemical change as our memories crowding into one another, we live all moments we have ever lived in the death trip.

Perhaps as we travel through our mythic reality (our cultural and personal narrative of what's happening as we die) towards the point of no return we have such a moment when time stops. The electro-chemical cycle of the brain breaks down as death happens and our awareness (viewed from a perspective outside the dying mind) ends. But our last subjective vision, whether it be of the universal light of peace and love, or alternatively of the horror at being extinguished, lasts forever. There may be no afterwards because we are dead; our narrative stops with this last unending experience, perhaps of heaven or of hell. Being open to this experience, and having magickally practised it, may mean the difference between which realm we subjectively inhabit forever in the afterlife.

Yet our treatment of the bodies of the dead may also be important, not least to the decaying consciousness. One of the great uncertainties of NDE is whether cognition and the formation of memories can happen after the electrical activity in the brain ceases. This could be an acid test for the 'hard problem' of mind/body dualism but gathering the evidence is, to say the least, tricky. What is surely the case is that even after electrical activity in our tissues ceases there are still deeper percolations of chemistry going on. Awareness may be contained to some degree in these final fluctuations. In many cultures mourners sit by the corpse, praying over it, dressing it, opening windows and turning mirrors to the wall. The lingering awareness gutters and dies like a candle but isn't finally snuffed out until days after we stop breathing. The work of the living is to help the dead rest in peace. Our bodies, themselves formed of elements created in dying stars, also dissolve back into the earth. Whether we choose burial by sky or water, fire, earth or air, the story in the long term is the same. We are taken up as nourishment for new life, over millions of years our organic traces may be folded deep within the earth, subducted into the fiery darkness. Our last gasp of air floats free, charged molecules of what once upon a time we would call 'me' may even evaporate into space. The way we treat the bodies of our dead says so much about our culture. Certainly it is one of the primary ways that the archaeologists of the future will attempt to re-construct what and how we believe. The spirit of a society leaves clues to its nature in the scattered mortal remains of its members.

Why do we die? At the roots of death is the fact that in the ancient earth there existed, as well as bacteria, viruses. These strange structures, tiny shapes that lock into cells, sometimes confer evolutionary advantages. But they can also alter the chemical cascade of life and become phages; disease. They feed on the DNA coded energy expressed in the cells life and destroy it, multiplying and spreading. Aeons before multicellular creatures existed our bacterial ancestors came up with a strategy. They deploy caspase-1 enzymes that race through the cell, killing it. In this way bacteria could die rather than let the phage spread. Uninfected cells would remain, some generating resistant progeny. In time the viruses would also mutate but once the tactic of death was established it could help life stay ahead of the game. Death is a strategy for life, and this applies at the most fundamental level of biology, not only when we get to the story of lions eating zebra. The life-force, Baphomet, has taken death inside itself. Billions of years ago the first eukaryotic cells emerged; they absorbed the mitochondria to be their power-house and hidden in those mitochondria was the mechanism of the caspase protein. Death waits coiled in the heart of all our cells.

A Serpent in the Garden.

So death is always with us. Like Castenada says, 'always at your shoulder'. Whether it is the memento mori on your desk, or the skin of your hands as you hold this book, we are always facing reminders of death. So is there a moral in this story? Does this magician's view of death tell us how we should live? Perhaps it tells us that death is vital to life. This may not stop us fearing death, or grieving; these are natural human processes. But it does help us see death as part of a larger story, as part of the narrative of Baphomet. And that tale is of a universe, which despite its apparent hurtling towards entropy, like an unstoppable juggernaut, also rises up into consciousness. That at every moment this awakening happens, as matter switches on awareness. That we should live both as though we were going on forever and, at the same time, as though any moment now we are going to…

Chains of Life after Death

A person dies. Those whose lives have been touched mourn, then pass into remembering why they mourn; the love, the kindness, the wise advice, arise again from cues found in the world around them. The acts of this dead person resonate through space-time, structures they built and words they said, hugs they gave, still altering the fabric of reality long after their physical biological body has passed away.

And the ripples of these acts continue for years after their name is forgotten. For the lives and objects they moved in turn move others, losing the identity of the individual's authorship, yet nevertheless carrying the touch of the person, and of those who touched and moved her.

In this current world of extensive records our names may stay attached to our creations and gestures for longer than in ages of purely verbal memories, yet our ancestors have no less of a memorial. We ourselves benefit from all the happy nights spent in company, the long treks to find food and water, the deep conversations around the fireside, the works of craft and art they delighted in. More, we only exist today because of these things.

Seeking for a kind of continued awareness after death from within one's biological vehicle may or may not provide fruit. Whatever the "truth" of such a quest however, we cannot help but be remembered, to influence, to advise, through the things we did when we were definitely here & now.

Death acts as a dynamic process, between the pauses we call Life. A release of energy held in a stable state, boundaries no longer maintained. The fluid muscles and tissues supported by the mineral bone structure, an inside out Cup, Death removes the perception of a body as a solid object, lets us see the liquid nature of our existence. Death, before, in front, and all around, the dark night beyond our hearths, the dark centre of every molecule; invisible and unseeable. Death does not mean cessation of movement, rather cessation of stasis.

La Santa Muerte, a deity I've worked with before, tells me things: She comes with kindness to bring rest, relief from pain, removes the broken and those injured beyond repair. Sometimes, she has people sent to her by others, this brings her sorrow, but she still meets these with equal kindness and acceptance. Practising for death, brings a life into full focus, recognition of the end means understanding of the story. Die well by living well, welcome death when you know it arrives. Each life a note, a humming resonance between the potential of the silent void, together making up the Song of Baphomet, ever changing.

Dredd Lord of the Shadows

Horned One, how long have I known you? I recall your shape as a carved antelope, elongated body and spiralling horns. Discovered in a charity shop, I enshrined your statue in my bedroom between trailing ivy plants. I made offerings to you as I lost my milk teeth: enamel and blood. I called you Rammastaff, my secret God, inspired by Saki's murderous tale of Sredni Vashtar. You were my childish religion.

Then I created you as a mask. Papier mache and black paint. I imagined your worshippers, we would be 'The Black Cult' and offer up wild dances and sacrifices to your name.

Your form seemed to call out at me from *2000AD* - the comic that is. I recall receiving the second issue and avidly reading the strip of Judge Dredd. This 22nd century lawman did his work hidden beneath a dark visored helmet. I remember going through that first story and adding what I felt was missing from the drawings of that character; horns.

I came to know your form as Levi's Sabbat goat, the icon of Karnayna depicted in esoteric picture books of intense looking Alexandrian Witches. And as I read more and more of the occult cannon I found you again and again.

Halloween 1981 and I am prepared. My room is darkened and huge tapers flame in the gigantic candlesticks I've created. My book of Shadows rests on the lectern, another item I crafted myself. On the altar (also hand-made) rests my athame, a chalice, and all the proper magickal paraphernalia.

I'm about to attempt my first invocation and assumption of a godform. I've read all the theory and been preparing myself with daily meditations on the attributes of my chosen deity. I've literally built the furnishings of my temple, and, importantly, arranged for my parents and sisters to be out until I've done.

The circle is cast and incense of storax and of patchouli hangs in the air. Clouds of it rapidly fill the room, spiral up from the cast iron cauldron in which the charcoal rests. I begin my invocations to Set.

Of course Set, Seth, the Egyptian Lord of the Darkness and Chaos, doesn't have horns, but instead the ears of an unknown species (strangely square, looking rather space-age I always think). But in my mind he occupied much of the same niche as the Horned Deity of Samhain. Moreover his bisexuality appealed to both my actual predilections and theoretical understanding of the liminal gnosis.

IAO IO IA SET, SETH, SHAITAN… holding my athame I spoke the invocation and the spell began to work. From my jaws a green, smoky crystalline snout began to form, those trademark ears (or were they antlers?) sprouted from my head. I felt my body enlarge, like a frog being inflated by a wayward schoolboy; my shoulders become huge corners of volcanic glass. My fingers grew long elegant nails of diamond sharpness. I was Set.

Fast forward to 1989. We are in a house in Lincolnshire, several witches, naked and dancing. It's Beltane and I am hunting, running with the herd, seeking the King Stag. The forest dances between my quarry and me. A dark haired sadhu (soon to become a leading light in the chaos magic movement, playing the part of the forest, hiding my quarry from me) expertly avoids my knife blade. But I am coming for that deer, my knife is raised again, the expectation of blood on the living room floor, but the High Priestess calls 'down!' The sadhu drops to the ground, the King Stag is still. His face is daubed ashen white and I am crowned with his antlers. Serpents are painted onto my wrists. The High Priestess and I perform The Great Rite.

Years later...I am falling, down into the earth. There is a tapestry in front of me composed of swampy greens, violets and indigo curved lights. These strobe and flood into one another, and the sound! The hissing of blood in my ears, the roaring of universes crashing into war. The sine wave of obliteration and recreation, and behind it all a growling bass note which shifts exponentially higher and higher, rising from the depths of the underworld to the pinnacles of the heavens.

It's overwhelming. I am not I, I am All! I am unfettered consciousness. And on the return I know that my form, my body, is the sensory organ of God, of Baphomet.

I believe that the experiences of altered states of consciousness, of gnosis or trance, allow us to perceive the deep structures of the universe. In an entheogenically inspired state, for example, we begin by noticing deep structures such as breathing, the saccading of our eyes or the presence of phosphenes. We can travel, beyond this enhanced sensitivity to our physiological activity, and get down to the root of consciousness. When we see trippy fractating patterns on, say, mushrooms, we are seeing thoughts, mental processes. The movement of these forms is the basic cognitive unit. Movement is the root of self-aware living systems, an amoeba can move towards something or away from something. When we see morphing patterns on psychedelics we are seeing the relationship of thoughts expressed through geometric kinaesthesia. The consciousness of the universe is the 'thing' that collapses the all-potential chaos into discrete beings (or rather 'doings' since the collapse gives rise to motion). This coming-into-being is what we see in trance. Our sense of time breaks down, the refresh rate of normal awareness changes and recursive perception folds in on itself; the fractal nature of reality is beheld.

Trance is how we learn. When we enter a trance state we become 'suggestible', that is we can learn more rapidly from a given input. Clearly this feature of the psyche can be used for good or ill. To heal or harm. People demonstrate reduced critical faculties when we are entranced. Trance is the tool of magick, of marketing, of propaganda and of dreams.

Whatever way they are arrived at (through ritual drama, dance, psychoactives or other methods) these altered states are a core feature of our biology. We can tell that we've always been this way. Today's archaeologists examine the material culture of ancient beliefs through the lens of neurophysiology. Decoding ancient cave paintings and rock art they have discerned the basic elements of the trance process. The shamans' journey of 10,000 years ago and of today arises out of the same neural wiring.

Baphomet for me is this self-conscious process of knowing the techniques and topography of the trance state. That's why there is the antinomian vibe in this figure. It is Lucifer, Promethea, and the Rebel in the Soul. Waking up to a religion in which mystical ecstasy and wonderworking are describable technologies rooted in the body. A religion in which physical sacraments are potent drugs that really do the job. A religion where we realise that we are God. And there is no God but Man.

Shamanism is an adaptation. A series of techniques that have evolved just the same way hands and eyes have evolved. Drumming, innerworld flight, psychoactives, the deployment of these techniques creates trance. In trance we can stimulate immunological responses at both an individual and cultural level. By perceiving the innerworld as spirits we extend our socialising simian style to the experiences that trance gives us access to. This isn't a dumb anthropomorphism but rather a seriously brilliant stratagem. Our brains are built to do complex social relationships. By perceiving thoughts not just as things but rather as entities we can open up channels of communication and control much more readily than if we stick to a farcical 'objective perception'.

This is why I conceptualise Life as the Great Spirit, which I call Baphomet. If you want to talk to something it's polite to address it by name.

So why the horns? Who knows? Perhaps it's the natural tendency of the mind to pay attention to the vertical symmetry of faces. The face I see on Baphomet is that of a V shaped form: Nemesis the Warlock, Herne the Hunter. Horns as a deeply embedded icon of power? (Well we've paid attention to horned beasts from before even Çatal Hüyük was built.) Horns as the basic duality arising from unity? Perhaps those horns are the fallopian tubes, or the shapes of plants? Or the simple yet profound mathematical fact that one gives rise to two, and then to many. A dendritic crown, like neurons or trees.

The Horned deity (which I insist on imagining as both male and female) is a real force emerging in the modern era, its emergence in occultism paralleled by technological and cultural change. Wicca has given rise to the horned god during the same period that nuclear energy and LSD were discovered. Tiny atoms that rise into whirling mushroom forms (both in the mind and over Japanese cities).

I speak as a shaman. A voice we can all share, a voice that can lead into collective consciousness for the good or ill of our species. The song sings through me, singing all creation into existence. And this act of creation is happening every instant. If the Big Bang happened before time then we might say that it is happening now, will happen. How can the unfolding of the universe be after an event that occurred before time itself?

I pray with tobacco. In front of me the sacred fire of the peyote circle is swept out into the form of a thunderbird. I pray that the sacred medicines can be used wisely and with right attention. I pray that we might soften the hearts of those who would forbid us such things. Great Spirit, whom I call Baphomet, hear my prayer!

Satan, Baphomet, Goddess of the World. Our work, the Great Work of Magick, is to wake up. Individually and as a species. Continuous Illumination; this is our Work! But this illumination is the whole process, entering trance and breaking it, and entering a new trance, a new way of being (and again breaking it…). Each time as magicians we move from state to state, trance to trance, we destroy a world. Like the Abraxas chick pecking out into the Mystery. Or as the Ancient Sage of Ankh-Morpork Mrs Cosmopolite would doubtless have observed, "you can't make an omelette without breaking eggs". It is this flow between states that we magicians Will embrace, riding the Shark of Desire through Manifestation.

The magician is the artist of the noosphere. The technician of the sacred. Combining elements of ritual to create specific forms of trance to open new possibilities of realisation. To do this work one needs core practice; yoga, meditation, to become skilful in the world. Then one needs to dare, to jump into the Mystery. For me working with Baphomet is like this. There is the silence between beats where we allow the resonance to unfold, time to listen to the universe. This is core practice. Then there are the beats, those rituals that strike trance induced meaning to the world.

A final memory. As I am led into the Chapel (the walls draped in banners of goats' heads, inverted pentagrams and eight rayed stars) I see what is on offer. A test. There is always a test and this time, as the Mass of Chaos B is chanted, I feel the possession take me.

Fig 11 Julian Vayne as Baphomet in Trafalgar Square as part of Antony Gormley's installation One and Other. Photograph by Simon Costin, 2009.

OL - SONUF - VAROSAGAI - GOHU

I - Reign - Over You - Saith

VOUINA - VABZIR - DE - TEHOM - QUADMONAH

The Dragon - Eagle - of - the Primal Chaos

ZIR - ILE - IAIDA - DAYES PRAF - ELILA

I Am - the First - the Highest - That Live In - the First Aether

ZIRDO - KIAFI - CAOSAGO - MOSPELEH - TELOCH

I Am - the Terror - of the Earth - the Horns - of Death

PANPIRA - MALPIRGAY - CAOSAGI

Pouring Down - the Fires of Life - On the Earth

Zazas, Zazas Nasatanada Zazas!

The White Darkness rises up and I am filled with animal intelligence, and rage and power. I am mad, manic, and insane. My vestigial self-awareness persists (now a pale ghost, tethered to a body filled with some unearthly force). There are voices; an offering is being made to Baphomet. It's shit, fresh and stinking. I'm squatting naked on a pew like a white gargoyle. My hands are long crystalline claws. The faeces do not smell repellent but rather of perfumed rich dark soil. Black Magick. My hands reach out; they grasp the excrement and smear it down my face and body.

Baphomet speaks.

"You in the circle with me, how lovely!"

Fig 11 Julian Vayne as Baphomet in Trafalgar Square as part of Antony Gormley's installation One and Other. Photograph by Simon Costin, 2009.

OL - SONUF - VAROSAGAI - GOHU

I - Reign - Over You - Saith

VOUINA - VABZIR - DE - TEHOM - QUADMONAH

The Dragon - Eagle - of - the Primal Chaos

ZIR - ILE - IAIDA - DAYES PRAF - ELILA

I Am - the First - the Highest - That Live In - the First Aether

ZIRDO - KIAFI - CAOSAGO - MOSPELEH - TELOCH

I Am - the Terror - of the Earth - the Horns - of Death

PANPIRA - MALPIRGAY - CAOSAGI

Pouring Down - the Fires of Life - On the Earth

Zazas, Zazas Nasatanada Zazas!

The White Darkness rises up and I am filled with animal intelligence, and rage and power. I am mad, manic, and insane. My vestigial self-awareness persists (now a pale ghost, tethered to a body filled with some unearthly force). There are voices; an offering is being made to Baphomet. It's shit, fresh and stinking. I'm squatting naked on a pew like a white gargoyle. My hands are long crystalline claws. The faeces do not smell repellent but rather of perfumed rich dark soil. Black Magick. My hands reach out; they grasp the excrement and smear it down my face and body.

Baphomet speaks.

> "You in the circle with me, how lovely!"

Years later I find myself in the heart of London. It is August 2009 and for one hour the fourth plinth in Trafalgar Square will be inhabited by Baphomet. I summon the guardians of the four directions; cover the platform with ivy and with roses. The bright, diffused light of the summer's morning turns my body into a black silhouette. The drum calls the spirit, the barbarous names of invocation are vibrated and Baphomet rises up, bringing the wilderness into the heart of the city. Throwing seeds from hir drum, Baphomet rains DNA down onto the earth. And dances and screams.

Alchemy

It all started with alchemy. Adding chemicals together to provoke psychological reactions (as we would frame it today) has been going on since before Homo sapiens existed. The favourite entheogen of the year for me is DMT. Apparently it is released naturally in the human brain (as in many other life forms) from the pineal gland, a scaly organ looking like a pine cone covered with eyes. All those drawings of phantastical monsters, thousand eyed, do they refer to the pineal gland? A friend saw their pineal gland whilst tripping, and they saw it look back at them. Several times lately, powerful visions have included as a key feature an eye looking back at me. An elephant's eye, a deer's eye, and in a dream I had, my own eye looked back at me through a sliding plate in a door that I then opened to me; myself and I.

These visions were spontaneous, not induced by perturbation of my neurochemistry centred around unusual material input or behavioural modification. I keep that kind of thing for rare occasions, lest the novelty aspect (essential for proper functioning of these odd states!) becomes too familiar.

By keying up our awareness to appreciate the world as our senses tell us, rather than from prior conclusions, entheogens and unusual actions (whirling, hanging, pain endurance, dancing to exhaustion) act on our intellect as well as our biochemistry (although some would say these represent two perspectives on the same phenomenon) to produce a fresh approach to the world, allowing a reset of established patterns. The neophiles amongst us relish and embrace this effect, the neophobes scream in terror. Given that we all contain elements of both traits, we can decide to reassure the part that clings to the familiar with cosy, reflective settings, while we encourage the elements we wish to clear themselves of kleishas by turning up the immediacy of sensorial awareness with enhanced environments/inputs, and further, we can provide access to both types of set at appropriate times depending on the trajectory of the journey through this spacetime to give all parts of us scope to flourish. The science and art of the psychonaut take a special kind of fool to practise even on oneself; attempting this kind of ritual as a group takes a special type of arationality coupled with deep roots of kinship built up over many shared experiences.

Entheogenic revelation has a role to play in our escape plan from historical baggage. By reaching epiphanies of present moment awareness, we build new foundations for what happens next. Leary's Turn On, Tune In, Drop Out message implying automatic success from ingestion of a chemical seems hopelessly simplistic these days, entheogens like other tools may get used to many ends. Nevertheless, with the plethora of consciousness altering techniques we now have access to within our culture, including trance inducing behavioural methodologies, we all have potential for achieving liberation from the threads of narrative causality which tie us to those mega fallacies of historical progress, industrial development, and other lumbering zombie institutions. We can collectively decide how we want our world to function. Books and the written rules tell us otherwise, but as we know, the written word has limited power when the audience looks up from the page en masse.

The Precious Toad Stone

"About 10 seconds or so after inhaling the last of the smoke, it began with a fast-rising sense of excitement and wonder, with an undertone of "Now you've done it," but dominated by a sense of, "WOW, This Is IT!" There was a tremendous sense of speed and acceleration. In perhaps 10 more seconds these feelings built to an intensity I had never experienced before. The entire universe imploded through my consciousness. It's as if the mind is capable of experiencing a very large number of objects, situations and feelings, but normally perceives them only one at a time. I felt that my mind was perceiving them all at once. There was no distance, no possibility of examining the experience. This was simply the most intense experience possible; a singularity, a white-out (as opposed to a black out), I have little memory of the state itself. I have no memory, for example, of whether my eyes were opened or closed. After some seconds or minutes, it started to fade and came to resemble a merely intense psychedelic state. Here I had the feeling, a visualization of being part of the universe of beings, all active in our daily, interwoven tasks, still moving at an incredible rate, and with a longing for a single group / organism awareness and transcendence. In a few more minutes it faded to an alert (+ one) state with an additional sense of awe and wonder, relief, and a strong feeling of gratitude toward the universe in general, for the experience."

The account above is drawn from Alexandra and Anne Shulgin's *TIHKAL* ('Tryptamines I have known and loved'). The magickal smoke that our informant has inhaled is known in the chemist's barbaric as:

#38. 5-MEO-DMT

TRYPTAMINE, 5-METHOXY-N,N-DIMETHYL; INDOLE, 5-METHOXY-3-[2-(DIMETHYLAMINO)ETHYL]; 5-METHOXY-N,N-DIMETHYLTRYPTAMINE; 5-METHOXY-3-[2-(DIMETHYLAMINO)ETHYL]INDOLE; N,N,O-TRIMETHYLSEROTONIN; N,N,O-TMS; BUFOTENINE METHYL ETHER; O-METHYLBUFOTENINE; OMB

The venom of the Sonoran desert toad is rich in 5-MeO-DMT and this has been the literal touchstone for much of the phase of the Baphomet work detailed in this book. But this volume isn't a grand tour of entheogenics and neither would we wish to single any medicine out for special status. There are many sacred herbs, mushrooms, animals and synthetic allies that can support us in our Work. What follows is simply an account of a specific ritual, The Circle of Baphomet, that was developed with the Divine Toad Venom as the engine to power the ceremony.

As Baphomet has many expressions so this is only one of hir rituals.

Naturally these experiments were all conducted in times and places where 5-MeO-DMT were perfectly legal; one should, when all said and done, never break The Law.

Baphomet Revisioned

Where to start? Chronological telling may not work. So much to tell... A need to see Baphomet for Real, that was the start, yes. Eliphas Levi long dead, his vision ancient and tired, wore out and unmoving. For me, and others, I felt Baphomet lived, and I needed a living Image/Icon to perceive the god/dess through; for a long time I felt this, growing with each invocation I did, the deity angry at the dumb animal scene.

I voiced this to Frater Salar, my magickal partner. He understood. We undertook vision quests, fuelled by our mutual desire, using sex and magickal practices. We talked for hours, we swapped photos, we looked for Baphomet as we walked our parts of the island. Exploring the Noospheric space of the planet, we got a perspective on the world and its enormous size. Baphomet, largest of the gods!

So what does sHe look like?

We saw, horns, but antlers and antelope wide-open horns, not the curled over goat.

The body we saw was human, the head switching and morphing into all other mammals, reptiles, the 2 eyed heads and brains of vertebrates.

In hir hands I saw snakes, one in each. One blue, one red/pink. Coiled into a double helix as they met in front of the genitals, stretching down into infinity. As Baphomet's hands moved, the colours linking the snake strands appeared – testing; some were broken again then reformed. The weaving of DNA forms, to mix up life and try Versions.

Baphomet, DJ of the biosphere. The Drumming track we often used to induce trance provided an on-off soundscape to the dance of life.

Creatures and power animals appeared, and I looked at the physical world around me to see what it looked like – what Life do I see each day?

Plants, yes – trees, many familiar landmarks, punctuating routes between home and elsewhere. Weeds in the cracks of man-made structures.

Irrepressible Nature.

Animals. I sat in the park, I saw a molehill moving. I felt how it is to live as a mole. A blackbird pecked for worms. A bee buzzed past the molehill, searching for flowers. Each creature only aware of others as it needed to be, as it needed to interact with them.

Except me.

Aware of all these, aware of the unseen billions of microbes in the soil, on the leaves. Insects and other invertebrates, some visible in fleeting glimpses. Aware of these creatures, and their awareness of each other. My world has so much more life in it than any other species.

Why?

Could this be what humans do – act to imagine the great web that connects all forms? The common link, DNA threads, stretching back in time to the first emergence of life 3.5 billion years ago. We look up facts and figures, the Interweb our mine of information, god Google sifting and searching.

Many emails, many conversations.

We feel moved by a current that we're part of. Synchronicities abound – the Noosphere the Biosphere the other Spheres of conceptualisation multiply.

In Temple K, we sit, with our other third, Soror Lilavirananda. We dive deep into other realms, questing for more visions. As one mind, we speak in unison, we can think together, linked in bodies and in astral space. We sway like waterweed in the swirling energies. Patterns show themselves to us. After one particular journey, I have to look further; I look down, down, so, so deep into the black hole of void consciousness. I see balls of colour; are they tiny? Or as large as galaxy clusters? Space or microcosm? Such beauty! I ask, for a sign of what I should notice, and a very small golden bead shines out. I speak my vision as I travel, my companions support my body, stroke me back to awareness, speak my words as I try to share my sight with them using sound to carry the pictures, return them from shamanic realms to mundane awareness.

Baphomet. Leviathan. In the Illuminatus! Trilogy, Robert Anton Wilson and Bob Shea tell of a deep-sea creature. One of two. It did not divide, it just grew, the protoplasm stuck together as One. The other of the two chose a different strategy – it pulled itself apart. Divided for love's sake, it endures the pain of separation from other life, to know all the better the pleasure of union. Frater Salar links this to the emotions of eating, of union via assimilation. Sex & Death.

We fuck, in many ways. As pairs of gods and goddesses, as ourselves, as magickal embodiments of ideals, swapping roles sometimes part way through so we each see both sides. Sometimes we lose track of whose leg or arm or thought or word or life is this? We always untangle ourselves afterwards though, entwined but nowhere attached; we meet and mix without dissolution.

A ritual. That is what we need – we want to share our living vision of Baphomet, the richness, the fluidity. The oldest of the gods and the youngest. Panphage, Pangenitor. The largest of the gods, and the smallest.

We write it together. A journey inwards, to connect our ability to see with our inner knowledge of Being Alive; to see for real the wonder of a cell, each one complete with DNA filled nucleus, unbelievably complex and self contained. The participants experience the four elements Earth, Water, Fire, Air. The manifestations of sacraments to represent each element present themselves: Soil. Water. Honey (energy solidified from sunlight). Plants (solidified air). Then, they encounter Spirit, directly perceiving Itself. We have a soft chant of the name 'Baphomet' and a drumbeat to hold the space-time rhythm. But how to manifest a sacrament of this experience?

Two weeks before we are due to perform this ceremony, the sacrament introduces itself via a merchant who attends one of Frater Salar's talks.

This gives us the medium we need to propel the participants into a deep state of altered consciousness. The toad has given us its philosophers' stone.

Credit must also go to all those around us who helped this process, via online and real time conversations, via writings and pictures, poems and songs. Our magickal colleagues who have shaped and worked with and listened to and manifested Baphomet over the years.

It all fits together.

Soror Res 369

Waves of time wash over me from past and future. Baphomet evolves.

A memory. We stand next to a pond, sunlight on our faces. We are holding hands. We look at each other and smile, we know without having to speak words what we want to do. We undress, we lie on the grass and the ground, beneath the trees, and we invoke Baphomet as god/dess of conjoined lovers, one deity in two bodies, the beast with two backs, we look into each others faces, each others eyes, as the sun shines from the sky above, we call each other names, we shout as the ecstatic state takes us and makes us into magickal life incarnate sky god earth goddess together.

We laugh at the absurdity of our pretensions afterwards of course, but in the following weeks whenever I look at the sky, I see my Lover's face. The echoes resonate still.

Toad in the hole, Whole in the Toad

Like most great magicks this one comes together as the confluence of many forces, emerging from the universe. In the same way that we become conscious of a face in the tree trunk, the human figures in clouds...

Baphomet for me is always the core image, a Mystery of Mysteries. The Eliphas Levi's goat of Mendes, a chimera of the elements, of human and animal, as above so below. The work that Res and I have put together weaves with Pete Carroll's Eschatological writings and his Chaos Jihad (developed online at Arcanoriumcollege.com).

To begin with the Baphomet form appeared in the tantra-at-a-distance that Res and I were working. 250 miles apart on different ends of this magickal island. Two forms intersecting; Shiva and Shakti, soil and sky. The first intention was to attempt a new conceptualisation of Baphomet, something that went beyond Levi's goat and all that Stygian darkness. A new god, the god of the Aeon that is incoming. Pete Carroll had been musing about the name for his 'new god' in his Eschatological work at Arcanorium, perhaps Tellus (an obscure earth deity from Classical myth). Res suggested instead, Baphomet, the natural choice; Io Baphomet, the Chaos magician's deity par excellence!

Perhaps like the way a crystal grows our work has developed according to its inbuilt plan. And this is apposite; Baphomet is the implicit order (or chaos...) the pregnant seed at the root of all things. For the biogram this is DNA, the twin serpents that underlie life on our world (and perhaps as distributed throughout the universe if the panspermia hypothesis is correct). The Horned God, my childhood obsession, Cernunnos, Herne, taken to the next level and integrated with my adult magickal self.

Into the Noosphere we went, Res and I, attempting to see, to feel the clues in that realm. We were looking for those strange attractors that could lead us to our future selves, to our most powerful and complete unfolding. And, like the Ouroboros serpent, we went right back to the start, to Liber Null and Psychonaut – to Baphomet.

As with much magick it wasn't that Baphomet wasn't already there, allied with our work. But it was the journey, finding out own way in the woods that lead to this 'new' formulation.

This was our first magickal child, the fusion of our work as occultists, as a magickal partnership, and I'm proud of our results. We'd created an invocation to Baphomet, 23 lines of poetry (one line for each human chromosome) to call on hir through many names and forms. Res cut this up and rearranged the text into a fantastically primitive and powerful incantation. From there we had developed a ritual for communing with the four elements. Plants, as forms of atmospheric carbon, for air. Honey (the medium that Res and I first worked with as part of our Mass of Maat working) for fire, water and soil for earth completing the picture. So we had our sacred text and a Eucharist but the proposal lacked a key ingredient. For Res and I, working with the tension of unfulfilled desire, that key was sexual energy. But how could this be expressed in a group setting? Sure one can organise orgies, and that is a perfectly excellent technique. But we were uncertain that this would be a suitable method, we were only aware that we needed an Engine for our Work.

The answer came with due synchronistic action. I was invited to attend a Pagan conference by the High Priestess of the Coven I'd been working with. I'd been asked to step in because the advertised speaker, who was due to lecture about the Holy Grail, had had an accident and couldn't be present. So instead the assembled company got me, talking about 'Aleister Crowley as Shaman'. After my lecture a curious individual buttonholed me. At our table (shared by two rather quaint pagan ladies) he told me that he was in possession of 5-MeO-DMT, a powerful psychedelic tryptamine. He handed me a leaflet about the substance and we began detailed discussions. A few weeks later I contacted this gentleman. 5-MeO-DMT is generally a synthetic derived chemical but it is found in nature in a few plants and, most famously, in the venom of the Sonoran desert (or cane) toad of North America. I drove to see my man. On my arrival he ushered me into his home. We made our way through the kitchen and into the sun lounge he had built at the rear of the property. The atmosphere was humid, almost tropical, as the sun beat down through the glass roof. My contact sorted me with 10 hits of toad venom. I declined his kind offer of smoking some then and there but stayed while he demonstrated the dosage and took a hit himself. After a few moments my host stumbled to the door and bade me good day.

A few weeks later in my temple I tried the material. Bang! This was it! Unlike N,N DMT this stuff was pure embodied tripping. Very little visual content, instead this was the sense and the definitely physical sensation of plunging into another world. Down the toad hole I travelled. My hands were pressed into the floor, my body curled up into a foetal position. Deeper and deeper into the earth, into the heart of things and at the same time the sense of expanding, being blown up, as large as the whole of the universe. I was in the core of reality, at the limitless extension of all that changes – I was one with Baphomet.

We had found the engine for our Baphomet rite. Frater Serpens Columba, Frater Pelagius and I were the first people to try the approach that Res and I concocted, with our new key ingredient. At the end of an excellent meeting we each took some of the four elements. We performed the yoga that Res and I had devised, a sequence of postures to stretch the body and affirm the divinity of the here and now, the transcendent as immanent panpsychism. I read the invocation that we had written. Frater Serpens Columba began to drum and Frater Pelagius to sing the name of Baphomet. No wild chant this one, worlds away from the style generally used in The Mass of Chaos B. Instead Baphomet's name was spun like sonic Sufi silk through the air. A comforting, swaying melody.

I took a big breath filled with the venom of the desert toad. All was one, the drum and lilting song carrying me downwards to the root of all. I was the serpent gnawing at the roots of Yggdrassil. The snake in the garden coiled around the Tree of Knowledge. Down I fell, and yet the solid form of my body bore me up. Like they say in qi gong 'the muscles fall, but the bones rise'.

We had something big here. Moreover for those not taking the sacrament the ritual was just as intense. Both the contact high phenomenon and the hypnotic drumming and singing would include everyone in the trance.

I experimented with the 5-MeO-DMT a few more times, becoming more and more convinced of the appropriateness of this ally to our work.

Weeks later; we are in the roundhouse; the walls are open to the forest. We have brought skins to sit upon, the elements to take as designed in the ritual, and the toad venom…

Res had yet to experience the sacrament. So she took a hit in the round house and closed her eyes. Too little, another, and I can tell by her reaction that she's got it this time. Down, down all the way down into the roaring centre of Pan, the all devourer and all begetter.

And so we are ready. The ceremony is the final one of the night. We led the company through what we had started to call the 'Horns of Baphomet' yoga. Then participants came forward to the centre of the circle. Here they received the four elements. Some settled back to chant and drum, others remained ready to undertake what I called 'the trance'.

There are many memories of those moments. Frater Axis looking around, mouthing words silently, a look of rapt astonishment on his face. One Frater, head down, moaning 'no, no, no'. Frater Kaitwm shaking like a man who had woken from sleepwalking, only to have discovered himself on the edge of a precipice. Soror Brigantia, laughing, Soror Lilavirananda laying on her back, arms and legs apart, opening and offering herself to the force of the trance.

What have we done? I hold the pipe up. A pile of black robes at my feet, some moaning, some giggling, some trying to return to their senses and singing again 'Baphomet, Baphomet…'. The cloud of octarine toad venom hangs in the temple. "Gods' tits!" I think, "I hope I haven't just killed anyone".

Luckily there were no fatalities and no lasting psychoses. At the end of the rite, for those who could stand, we stood in a circle and opened out the space, releasing the energy of our experience into the world. Chaos Magicians to the last, this process has a definite intent, a definable result; namely that the people in the rite, and all those they touch would begin to feel their lived connection to the earth. Our aim was (and is) that rather than just thinking about, or intellectually knowing our relationships in the biosphere, it should be felt, and felt intensely. That this feeling should contribute to our sustainable unfolding as a species. Feeling ourselves rooted deep in the earth, we reach for the stars.

> "The toad, while ugly and venomous, yet wears a precious jewel in its head".

During the ceremony I had anchored this intention. "This feeling"' I had said as people travelled in the trance "is what we call Baphomet".

We had tested our ritual. Improvements were made, upgrades to our process. A new element was introduced, the idea that as participants moved into the circle, before sampling the elements, that they should become aware of the process of evolution on our planet. Spiralling towards the centre where the sacrament lay, the magicians would be asked to become aware of the staggering duration that life dwelt as single celled organisms on our earth, before the gradual and exponential development of more complex forms. With mammals and hominids occupying the tiniest sliver of geological time.

So for an international meeting of magicians we have the process ready. To the beat of a slow drum, we walked silently to the site of the ceremony. A brilliant gap in the weather permitted us to work outdoors, something Res and I had enchanted for. In a ritual circle of thirteen sacred trees we had made our space. Animal skins and mats in the centre. Drums and other equipment ready, the four elements; plants, honey, water and soil.

The Horns of Baphomet yoga loosened up our participants and they began to walk in a spiral, moving inwards, across billions of years of evolution. In the centre they arrived at Now, the heart and fullest extension of evolution on our planet. Taking the elements, some remained seated in the centre, others withdrew and continued to chant and drum. Soror Lilavirananda and I dosed all those Brothers and Sisters who knelt in the centre of the circle.

And it was good.

They travelled into the trance, watched over by guardians who would support and care for them. Safe so that they could, without fear, lose themselves into the feeling, the feeling that we call Baphomet.

Laughing and amazed people emerged. The sky was blue, the sun bathed us with golden rays.

> "And at the end of this ritual" declared Soror Res. "We use the Mithraic salute of fellowship". She and I demonstrate by shaking hands. The party erupts; clasping hands, embracing, kissing, talking and laughing. Baphomet is everywhere.
>
> "Like little children, oh yes" says Frater KaterKarlo (The last person to undertake the trance). "Laughing like children!"

Later Soror Onca tells me her story. She felt fear, lost and confused by the trance, until she reached out and grasped the grass beside the sheepskin upon which she was kneeling. She opened her eyes and saw all the way down into the DNA. "It was then I really understood why I'm a biologist," she said.

The Hidden God/dess has awoken!

Frater Salar 217

Deep Baphomet

I draw deep. The otherworldly smell of the smoke fills me. Everything is dark. I am kneeling, I've put myself in child pose, feel the reassuring wool of the sheepskin beneath my hands. My mind's eye falls further down, into, I see nothing but nothingness. Red lines, red darkness, start to link. Tessellated pentagrams, a geometrical impossibility, pulse. Remember to breathe, I think, not in words but in an urge to inhale and exhale; I fear I may forget to breathe, I know fundamentally that I am about to lose all sense of body. So, I keep up the slow murmuring song of 'Baphomet, Baphomet, Baphomet…', a chant that for a long while forms the only co-existing event between my internal and external sense of self. The inner visions stay simple for a while then develop, revealing the forms that have evolved from our unicellular ancestors. Familiar as I am with this story, seeing it in multi dimensional form takes me by surprise. I, as a person, identifies with I Baphomet, a place I've visited many times before in various states, both under the influence and from purely behavioural modifications to my mentations. I settle in to this double existence, for me a reassuring fit.

I speak, and I listen.

Divided for Love's sake, I Live as all things. Folded and kneaded together my flesh shaped itself, pushing and pulling in a dance with itself and the World, lead and leader, choosing both paths at every junction. I tore myself apart to see the world's ways. I touch the whole face of the planet, oozing into cracks, reaching up to the skies, perceiving and fuelled by so many, many sources. Fountains of exuberant abundance leap up when the chemistry is right, when the moment comes. Carpets fill the rooms of my lands, furnished with comfortable resting places, familiar routes to travel, green swathes all. Invisible to some eyes I burrow in beneath apparent wastes, divers strategies and forms as I eat the very rock. And, in the water, oh the water! My forever home, so empty and so full! Vast tracts with nothing but dead substance, swirled through with rivers of blooming creatures, spirals run hot and cold transporting their contents across oceans, the waters I Love.

The voice fades, and I realise I have been continuing to chant throughout this vision. I open my eyes to a world at once the same and brand new. I look up, meet the sparkling eyes of my Brother, and we see ourselves. We smile. He offers me water, saying 'May You Never Thirst', our tradition's words. We talk, I tell a bit of my journey, bringing back the relevant pieces of knowledge to my mundane world. Honey tastes sweet like never before.

After a few minutes to adjust, I stand, and walk out of the roundhouse; we carry the sheepskins back to our room in the main building. My vision has returned to normal, yet a lingering sense of new-ness still makes each leaf and branch, each insect crawling or flying, and my own body even! appear as a marvellous product of its environment, billions of years in the making. The way a spider web fits onto twigs, now looks ancient and like the first morning simultaneously. Centred firmly back in my usual sense of body, within half an hour we are sitting at the kitchen table with cups of tea, chatting normally with some friends.

Stories from
The Circle of Baphomet

"Fell forward with lattice of green crackly lights.

A huge groan swelled around me from outside and I fell through, or into something which was black and very, very cosy. Expansion. My body was nowhere.

Tall white alien figures were present. They were a group, a council, keeping order, but there were no laws, just gentle nature. There was a strong physical sensation of being cosseted, held all over. Perhaps like being in a warm bath, but the water pressing.

The figures were more colour than beings, individuals but joined.

One of them said a word (I'm keeping it to myself) in a whisper, as if not to disturb anything, like after a refreshing drink. The sound flowed through the space appearing as coloured light, like a rainbow in oil. It bounced off the 'sides' and back to the others, who fed on it and returned with their own word. Most gentle, like whalesong.

I saw the colours and how the bounced and said a long, deep and hard "No". My voice stretched. It was a long 'no'. The waves of colours bounced and rippled, still smooth, but fast.

The others countered by smoothing the 'no' out. I said 'no' a few more times, just 'cos I wanted to see what would happen. They didn't react with anger, but I felt so much (here goes) love.

I heard the Baphomet chant and the banish with laughter and emerged."

*

"Suddenly as I could hear the sounds of chanting around me I realised how funny it all was, there I was on a Saturday night, in the middle of the woods surrounded by people wearing black robes all chanting tunefully "Baphomet", it all become funnier and funnier, - the whole situation was unbelievably funny. I then realised that this laughter was the manifestation of Baphomet. I could feel my magical Brothers and Sisters inside my head, some individuals manifested inside my head more strongly than others, but the whole community was there. I could feel a pressure on my head, like fingers going inside my brain making circular patterns at the crown of my head and I could feel the mantra spiralling into my brain.

I saw a vortex, I had a choice of whether to go in or not but I could hear the mantra encouraging and urging me to do so. I knew the members of the Temple were there and thought "oh well in for a penny in for a pound" and dived into the vortex.

I saw my life and the things in it that were important to me and found that it was all unbelievably funny. I saw my death and as I watched myself dissipating into nothing ness, I almost died laughing, and as I saw myself laughing at myself as I watched myself dying I laughed! I thought I would never stop laughing!

It was like seeing my life and the world from the outside and from the outside there's a lot to laugh about!

All of the images were in black and light and there was no colour.

I saw the universe, I saw it come into being and then I saw it being destroyed, I saw this over and over... and laughed over and over and suddenly all that was there was laughter there was nothing else. It went silent and I could hear a voice saying, "This is the real Baphomet."

I then saw the most terrifying image of Baphomet I have ever seen and as I looked at the image and it shattered into many small pieces. Then there was silence.

I could feel myself being pulled up onto my feet, and I recall asking the question "What the fuck was that".

The ritual was having all beliefs dismantled in one fell sweep. I didn't know quite what to do with this afterwards… talk about "all the kings horses and all the kings men." I could not be sure if I was really here for some time after the ritual.

Since then I have reconstructed a belief system somewhat as I need some things around me to stay sane, for example, to believe that I'm here is very useful - but while I choose to believe some things these beliefs are wrapped around me like a coat and underneath there is a small voice going "ha!!!"

The ritual did not last 10 minutes it lasted for months as I found myself being pulled into the experience several times afterwards, and waking up at night having dreamt of falling into holes. As time went on the holes ceased to be black and light and become very colourful, sometimes I had them while awake.

*

This time I took less and felt myself being pulled into a hole in the ground, and I could hear the mantra fading as I went into the whole. In the whole it was like experiencing a cosmic organism and a sensation of feeling the heart beat of creation. I had a sensation of merging and any sense of self-dissipating.

Since then I have had odd falling through holes dreams but they are easier to work with than the last ones. The first experience of the ritual had a feeling of disconnecting and my second experience was more of connecting.

*

I smoked the DMT through a glass pipe, and then adopted a foetal position with my forehead to the ground. Sensations seemed to shimmer for a few seconds, and I felt a little euphoric. I asked for more in the hopes of intensifying these effects. I took a much deeper lung-full of the smoke the second time round and resorted to my supplicatory position. Instead of an intensification of the previous effects a completely new and unexpected experience emerged.

My awareness seemed to move out of my body in a backwards and expansive fashion, while my body felt very heavy and grounded. The resulting 'reality' seemed much more vivid and real than the normal everyday trance. It felt unitive, although there was an element of confusion as to where I ended and other phenomena (such as the ground and other people) began. The state was euphoric and sensual with a highly visual aspect – lots of geometric patterns, occult symbols and colours. The state seemed to encourage the making of sound. I let out a big laugh, before finding myself making 'ahhhhh' sounds as I employed some connected breathwork to open myself up to the experience. The state had both a divine and organic quality to it (I wonder if the organic 'life' quality had anything to do with Baphomet?). What I normally call 'Alan' wasn't there anymore – it was as if I had been scrambled and mixed with the surrounding environment, people and visions. I could see how this had the potential to be terrifying or panic inducing, although I felt neither.

Time during the state seemed to last very long, although the experience was more or less over after 10 minutes. I felt clear afterwards, as if someone had hit my reset button. There was a pleasant 'hangover' of the experience that lasted a few days.

I feel I need to stress just how intense this experience was; it took me a good few days or so to reach the above description, and I'm convinced the experience had something to do with death, although I have no idea how.

*

I found it to be a very beautiful way to get in contact with Baphomet and more!

The soft chant from the circle created a smooth path into something very special.

I took a very small amount of the "toad", still this was enough to do quite some things....

I guess the visuals I had were not due to the "toad" (as the amount I took was small), but the toad created a very strong physical, bodily perception of my journey.

It was great to work outdoors (which I generally enjoy a lot) and especially in the environment you created. The setup was very supportive for the purpose of the work.

*

With the wave of the sacrament I became very conscious about the organic world around me, experiencing it in a physical way - touch-feel-taste-smell sensors were all busy.

The soft chant created a groove into the matter (as after the sacrament I wasn't laying really on the ground).

Following the groove I descended, or such was the feeling, but it wasn't a descent into the ground, it was more of a descent into the scale of things.

It was similar to a Baphomet invocation, as this was the consciousness I met. But while in a Baphomet invocation I usually become (more or les) Baphomet and thus "contain it all in me", this time I was more of a particle and very aware of the big Baphomet, who I was experiencing from the inside....

All in all the experience was very pleasant for the mind, but very challenging for the physical body.

*

Checked with my spirits, and 5MeO is a different spirit to NN, and it's OK to give it a go.

Sucked in a lot, on a final impulse. Kept telling myself to let go, surrender, and at some point the spirit voice said: Don't do ANYTHING. Let go or it will really hurt. The painful moments were warnings. I rode out a storm of energy, in a place like the outdoors I was in, but with torrents of power running all around and through me, to the background sound of the beautiful Baphomet chant and sounds like someone orgasming.

At some point, I applied the question I've used before in extreme states: 'If I knew I was dying now, would I do the same as I'm doing?' And the answer was yes, which I always take as a good sign.

Deliciously spaced afterwards.

*

Outside as we started to move in a circle, chanting, the need to feel the earth under my feet was pleasantly insistent, and the result of getting rid of shoes and socks was immediate. The feeling of grass and earth under my feet sent me even further into a very pleasant (relative) disorientation. Which was perfectly enhanced, supported and intensified by the Baphomet mantra

After taking the sacrament, a chain reaction started…

The image I had in my minds eye (a freeze frame from my immediate surroundings pre-sacrament) fractalised, remained fixed just long enough that I could focus on it, then immediately fractalised and multiplied again, stopped, I focused on it again, and again my focusing was the trigger for immediate further fractalisation and multiplication. This at a fantastic rate of acceleration, faster, wider, … until at some point it became a continuous process which evolved into what I can describe as a starburst (?) an enormous explosion of light which became countless golden points. These points settled each into their own particle (subatomic atoms? genes?) at the point of the explosion and what followed it, I fell into it. The impression was that at that moment I was those points of golden light, in every atom, every gene, every molecule , that I was part of everything, and exactly in that same moment that I didn't exist any more. I was nothing and part of everything at the same time. It was a deeply satisfying and reassuring state of being and very familiar… "Remember? " or something in that direction…

At some point I became aware of two very large friendly beautifully ornate eyes smiling at me that was the point that I returned and saw Soror Cows smiling and some other people looking a bit concerned.

*

Fig 12 *"Axis of sky and land and sea. In every blade of grass, every day's eye."* The Eyes of the Day, photograph by Nikki Wyrd.

Horns of Baphomet yoga

Stand with feet shoulder width apart. Hands lightly touching, middle fingers on your navel. Looking straight ahead, a level gaze at the distant horizon. Inhale; raise your eyes to the sky, keeping the head still. Open your heart area.

Exhale slowly, bend to the ground from the head downward, folding forwards from the waist, letting the arms drop easily. As the hands touch the ground in front of the feet, pause briefly. Inhale again as the hands trace two lines from the earth to the toes, up each leg, to meet again at the navel; hold the breathing at this point. The hands continue their motion upwards, together now, till they reach the heart. Here they move apart to each shoulder, start to exhale very slowly as the hands leave the body, and raise the arms up to the sky, reaching out to space in a gesture like the algiz or maðr rune. The gaze is upwards, with the head still facing straight ahead, as at the start. Float the hands down and around, bringing them back to the starting place at the navel. Pause, before taking another breath, thus repeating the cycle, if necessary.

When you've done this enough, go and do something more interesting.

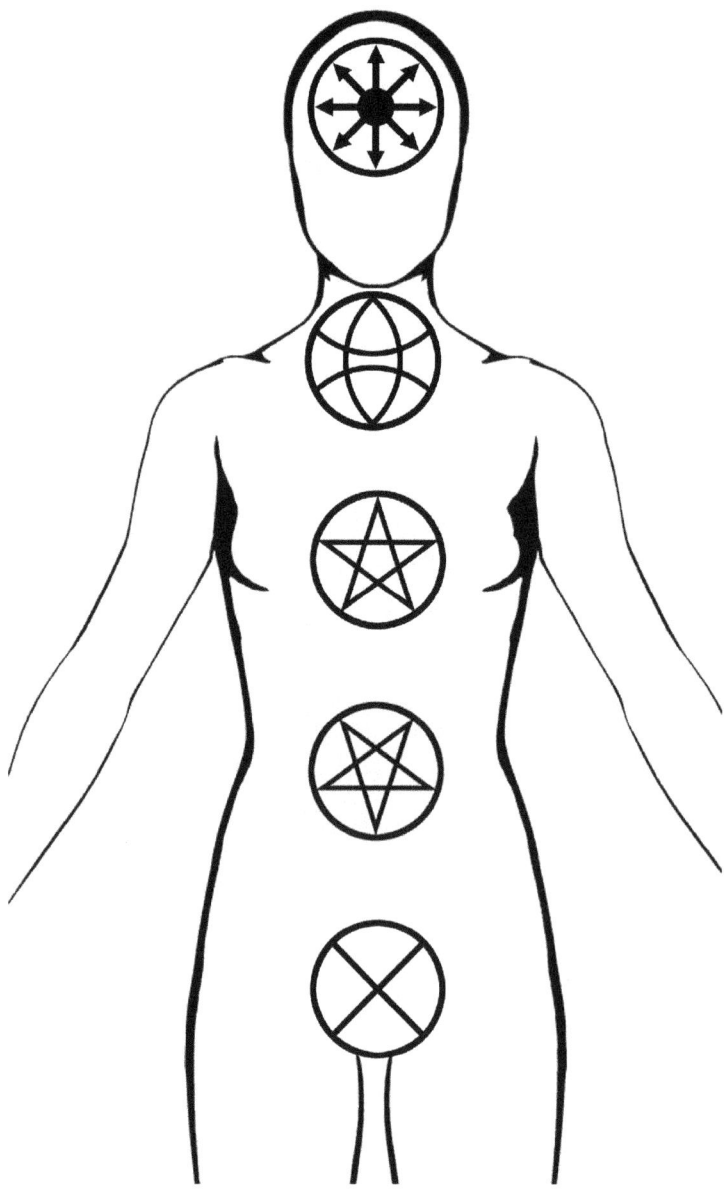

Fig 13 Symbols of the Gnostic Chaosphere Rite by Frater Tadhg.

Gnostic Chaosphere Ritual

(GCR) first published in Arcanoriumcollege.com developed by Frater Stokastikos with assistance from Soror Res.

Frater Stokastikos writes:

I E A O U

Panpsychosphere

Noosphere or memesphere

Anthrosphere or Opusphere

Biosphere

Geosphere

I
Panpsychosphere

The Panpsychosphere. As magicians and sorcerers and shamans we need to entertain the Panpsychic Hypothesis, the intuition that all phenomena behave in animate fashion to some degree (depending on their quantum characteristics in my view). This, or something like it, constitutes the basic inductive leap from observation or experience that makes us magicians.

The Panpsychosphere which we can represent with the Chaos Star; implies all possibilities including apparent impossibilities, the realm of the aethers (or quantum waves) where material reality branches into multidimensional Apophasis and where Apophasis occurs in which unreal events subtend real effects into the lower worlds. The Panpsychosphere represents the realm of cosmic imagination from which emergent phenomena arise spontaneously and chaotically in all the lower spheres and which stimulates personal creativity. Perhaps that barely makes sense in words, and the maths looks even worse, but maybe it conveys the intuition to some extent.

The Panpsychosphere stands above even the Noosphere. Whilst the Noosphere represents all existing memes and ideas and these memes and ideas also have a footprint in the Panpsychosphere, the Panpsychosphere also represents the source of all ideas and all emergent forms that may yet come into existence.

E
Noosphere or memesphere

The Noosphere, sometimes called the memesphere, represents the sum of all ideas, beliefs, religions, philosophies, emotions, hopes and terrors arising from all structures capable of creating them. This primarily seems to arise from more complex organisms such as ourselves, but we should not discount the possibility that some of it may arise from other creatures, nor the speed and volume with which information and ideas now travel through our electronic media. The noosphere probably already contains many of the secrets of life the universe and everything, plus vast numbers of useless answers and downright toxic nonsense as well.

Increasingly it seems like the battlefield on which the fate of the Anthrosphere hangs. In the GCR we can symbolise it with the sign of the Tellus, an obscure astronomical symbol for the earth which suggests ideas converging, diverging, and overlapping.

A
Anthrosphere or Opusphere

The Anthrosphere, sometimes called the Anthroposphere or Opusphere, represents the biomass of humanity and its reticula (all that it has made in terms of structures and manufactured items and modified environments for itself). The upright pentagram representing a human spread-eagled as in the microcosmos of Vitruvius and in Leonardo's drawings symbolises this sphere.

The anthrosphere has evolved from the biosphere and remains critically dependent on it and on the geosphere, yet it now becomes apparent that we have started to inflict serious damage on both.

O
Biosphere

The Biosphere, all living biological organisms from algae and bacteria to whales and mighty trees, including us. Basically this consists of a thin layer penetrating only a few tens of metres into the soil and a few hundred metres into the sky, although it has greater thickness in water.

The sophisticated image of Baphomet by Levi resumes plant and animal and human symbolism and hence we can use its simplified pentagramic form with two points upward here. The biosphere has obviously evolved from the geosphere and the Gaia hypothesis strongly suggests that the biosphere has modified the geosphere to meet its evolving needs.

U
Geosphere

The Geosphere, basically the apparently inanimate planet itself, this of course includes the lithosphere (rocks), hydrosphere (waters) and the atmosphere, plus the energy sphere, both in terms of the fiery core and the energy inflow and outflow with space. The symbol of a circle in a cross represents a traditional astrological sign for earth and also the quarters of earth, air, fire, and water comprising the planet.

Directions

0) Grasp the magical weapon; prepare to use it to trace the symbols over the body and in the air. (If performing this ritual for Chaos Jihad purposes)

1) Choose metaphysical east, (any direction at whim).

2) Inhale and vibrate on the outbreath 'I', whilst visualising the chaos star in the brow. This symbolises the Panpsychosphere, the sum of all possible wave functions (aethers) arising from all animate structures on earth whether apparently sentient, animate or inanimate.

3) Inhale and vibrate on the outbreath 'E', whilst visualising the symbol of the Tellus in the throat. This symbolises the Noosphere, the sum of all ideas, emotions, hopes and fears arising from all structures capable of giving rise to them on earth.

4) Inhale and vibrate on the outbreath 'A', whilst visualising the symbol of the upright Pentagram in the heart, the sign of humanity. This represents the Anthrosphere, the sum of humanity and all the physical structures that it has created on earth.

5) Inhale and vibrate on the outbreath 'O', whilst visualising the symbol of the Baphometic pentagram, (two points upward) in the solar plexus area. This represents the Biosphere, the totality of biological life on earth.

6) Inhale and vibrate on the outbreath 'U', whilst visualising the symbol of Earth in the genital-peritoneal area. This represents the Geosphere, the rocks and waters and atmosphere of the planet.

7) Repeat steps 6 to 1, working back to the power point in the brow.

8) Draw and visualise a Chaos Star ahead, intoning the IEAOU mantra and drawing the 4 intersecting lines carrying the eight arrows (in any

preferred order) each to the sound of one of the first four sounds, finally complete the centre circle to the 'U' sound.

9) Turn 90 degrees to the left and repeat step 8 to the next quarter.

10) Continue and do the same to the other two quarters and return to metaphysical east.

11) Repeat steps 1 to 7.

12) Remain silent for a few moments and strive for void-mindedness.

13) Laugh and relax, or go about the next magical operation.

As with all rituals, participants should familiarise themselves with the meanings attributed to all symbols beforehand and then concentrate solely on the symbols themselves during performance to achieve maximum sleight of mind.

Note on using the GCR 1.8 version and other variations

Further variations on this banishing ritual have emerged from the praxis of group development. These include, removing the repetition of the pillar of sound vibrations (Step 11), on the grounds that this repetition acts as a 'double negative' on mundane reality, leaving the banishing banished. Variation 1.8 sees this single pillar of sounds combined with the Chaos Stars drawn to eight directions, rather than four, creating a more circular feel to the ritual.

Fig 14 Baphomet by Frater Fux.

Baphomet Through the Spheres

O Baphomet! Oldest of the gods, and the youngest! I call upon you to guide my path, to inspire my words with the Wisdom of Ages, the Spirit of this Present Time, that your presence shines through these pages for years to come. Baphomet, lend me your poise, your power, that I may better express the utter joy of each transient moment as a part of your senses! Bless the passage of this work, that it finds those who need it most.

In 2011, I put into written words a formal scheme, describing a suggested method of leading up to an Invocation of Baphomet. Originally distributed as an online course at Pete Carroll's Arcanorium College, where I presently have the honour of the title of Vice Chancellor. The material reproduced here formed the basic instructions, with further conversations between myself and the rest of those following the invocation process taking place over a period of six weeks. The spheres of the GCR indicated to me a set of perspectives from which to approach this deity of our world, this larger than life character, bigger than the sum of parts; yet by starting from the parts one can make an attempt at grokking the whole. I cannot stress enough that there exists no hierarchy, nor nesting of these spheres. They represent, in my mind, simply different perspectives from which to view the object of our attentions. One would not claim a tree to be a nested set or a hierarchy of biological, chemical, physical, poetical, artistical, cultural or historical descriptors. One simply uses the most appropriate terminology to the situation at hand, which then calls forth the most suitable and valuable method. The tree itself remains the same tree throughout this process, only our own limited observations change.

Before getting to the course material, I must warn you that jumping straight in to this type of magickal practice without a bit of a run up could prove tricky. Do a few months meditation, absorb the rubric of a good banishing ritual or two, and learn how to concentrate, prior to attempting a full-on possession style invocation.

Week 1 Geosphere

Life from the viewpoint of the rocks.

> "It is well known that stone can think, because the whole of electronics is based on that fact, but in some universes men spend ages looking for other intelligences in the sky without once looking under their feet. That is because they've got the time-span all wrong. From stone's point of view the universe is hardly created and mountain ranges are bouncing up and down like organ-stops while continents zip backwards and forwards in general high spirits, crashing into each other from the sheer joy of momentum and getting their rocks off." Terry Pratchett, *Equal Rites*.

Earth. Our planet, spinning through space. Inside, molten rock. A thin, hardened crust, covered with a living semi permeable membrane we call soil. This part of the ground lives. The crust below now mainly consists of what has lived. Once it was mere chemical/mineral matter (choose you own favourite terminology), but after 3.5 billion years of living organisms, the turnover of the tectonic plates has resulted in a rocky crust made from bits of creatures, bits of old mountains, bits of ocean floors and seashores.

Only the very oldest rocks contain no fossils, no contribution from Baphomet's own body.

Everything else we stand upon, from the bottom of the ocean to the top of the highest mountain, consists of death, a mixture of old life forms and old rocks.

Baphomet, oldest of the gods.

Baphomet, god of Death.

Exercise 1

One morning this week, leave your house early and make a 5-10 minute stop somewhere on or close to your normal route to work (or equivalent). Undertake the last part of your journey on foot, rather than getting out of a car straight on to it. Walking massages the ground beneath you, activating the acupressure points of our Mother Earth (according to something I read once). If you can walk all the way, even better.

Upon arriving at the location you've chosen for your appreciation of what supports you, simply observe the environment. See the shape of the land, note any actual rock you may see, and feel the solidity beneath you. Look at the plants, see the minerals that comprise parts of many of their molecules, and feel the resonance of this image with the minerals within your own body which have entered you from plants/plant eating animals.

Without the mineral elements hard won from the parent material beneath the soil, Life would not stand as it does.

Take a few minutes to consider these concepts in the place you have chosen.

Exercise 2

Spend 10 minutes (or more) researching the names of the mineral elements within your body that have come from rocks, from the geosphere. Make a note of these if you wish.

E.g. Iron (Fe)- Found in haemoglobin, a protein essential for carrying oxygen in the bloodstream.

Please share your results from these exercises with the class via your diary thread, and feel free to comment on other students' posts too. Photographs and other media add further depth to your records.

Exercise 3

Cast a circle in your favourite way.

Lying flat on the floor, meditate upon the ground for a short while, I suggest a good twenty minutes but, I appreciate a lot of people fall asleep in this position quite easily, so if you start to feel your attention wandering too far from the ground, better to finish the session rather than go too far adrift from the object of concentration.

After you have done this enough, eat some hearty food.

Drink some water.

Keep the last portion of the food and water, and at a convenient time take these remains to the place you visited in the first exercise, and leave them on the soil, the living fractal boundary between above and below. Speak to the place, either aloud or in thought, giving attention to the spirits of the place.

Banish with laughter at appropriate points during these works.

Week 2 Biosphere

This week we explore the aspect of Baphomet most familiar to us, the perspective of Life on Life.

Everything alive perceives. It's one of the most basic standard characteristics of a living organism. For the record these are usually listed as cells, homeostasis, heredity, use of energy, reproduction, response to the environment, and evolution & adaptation. To respond to the environment, you need to perceive it in some way, however simply.

You, reading this, perceive as a human animal. Other animals perceive in their own way. Obviously... What else you need to appreciate though, centres on the way that what leaps to attention in the environment changes as your internal mood shifts, whether in response to previous external stimuli, or internal chemical signals.

And this is true for other organisms too. In addition, they have different sensory organs. Some are so similar to ours that we can assume a near match of the signals possible to perceive, e.g. a cat can see your food as cat food. Not in colour, admittedly, but you get the idea.

Baphomet comprises the egregore of all organisms, all life. SHe perceives in all the ways they do. From my decades of experience, invoking and watching other people invoke this godform, Baphomet can appear in many various moods. Sometimes, the mood that turns up does not match the expectation of the invoking person, which has led to events that we have later laughed about...

Bearing this in mind, try to avoid slipping into a possession state during this week's work. We have a long way to go before the invocation proper. Baphomet does not equate 1:1 to the horned god of the beasts.

If you have not already at some point in your life thus far done so, do a bit of research into the wildlife of your location. Then, look into how these types of animals and other organisms perceive their world; even plants react to light, for example, and can distinguish between shade cast by rocks or buildings, and that from another plant, allowing them to respond with appropriate reactions (e.g. in the shade of a competing plant, they strive even faster to outgrow the sunlight thief next to them, whereas a cliff provokes growth of larger leaves to catch more of what light is available). Many of the microscopic organisms can detect gradients of chemicals and minerals in the soil, prompting growth of their mycelium towards phosphorus rich zones.

This doesn't need to be exhaustive, just get a couple of examples you can use to spread out the appreciation of the many ways life feels into its environment. Migratory birds have a magnetic field sense, and see in a range that includes our own plus near UV.

Here in the northern hemisphere at the moment, this exercise will prove less rewarding than in the summer months. However, I tried it out the other day, and it still provided me with many impressions. Mostly bird and plant based I admit, the invertebrates and mammals were hiding out of sight!

I realise we here only touch on one aspect of the shared characteristics of Life. We have only one week, and many of these would be hard to detect even within our own bodies let alone in those of others. Please add in any way of grokking them if you can find a way, and share with us your experiments!

Exercise 1

Find a place outside that you can sit undisturbed and unself-consciously. If necessary, use a ruse or two to disguise your real purpose; smoke a cigarette, hold a book as if reading it, pretend to be asleep, look like you're taking photographs (an excellent excuse to be staring around at nothing in particular without appearing crazy...).

Use your human sensory abilities to describe the place to yourself. Take a few minutes to go through as many of the senses as you can.

What other organisms have you become aware of during this time? Which of them can you directly sense, which appear from signs they have left?

Take a while to consider, as each organism comes to mind, what the sensory world of that organism could tell it about the world, what part of that information we understand, and which parts we can never directly know as human animals.

In particular, consider how the organisms you grok perceive other organisms.

Remember to include non-animal organisms.

This could potentially take a very long time, so just continue for as long or short as you wish.

Banish with laughter.

Make sure you have solidly returned to your own person by reciting the mantra of the fully normal, "My name is [ordinary given name], I live at [postal address]".

Exercise 2

(You can follow on soon after exercise 1, although I think a pause of a day or so would help to assimilate the first impressions.)

At the same place, go through exercise 1 in a fast forward kind of remembering way.

Step back from your physical involvement in the scene; look objectively at the many organisms present, including yourself. Now consider, if you were Baphomet, the collective awareness of Life, which organism best allows you to manifest this godform? Which of those present can imagine/appreciate the myriad impressions? If you were Baphomet, what would an organism that could run this kind of activity need to have as attributes and physical properties (sense/processing capabilities)?

Banish with laughter.

Exercise 3
(Optional, but recommended!)

Repeat 1 & 2 as above, but for a wider area; the piece of land you reside on, the continent, the planet. Do this exercise in a place you feel very secure, as it can mean quite a long period of deep trance.

N.B. The average lifetime does not allow enough time to complete this exercise fully, so an approximation may be all you can manage.

Banish by doing something that gives you immediate physical pleasure, of whatever type you can achieve best in your surroundings.

Week 3 Opusphere

Otherwise known as the Anthrosphere.

The works of Man. Physical, geoengineering and land use change, farming, urban, roads, mining, water structures, alteration of the atmosphere, engineering, art works, writing, sound engineering, light control, heat control, tools, machines, craft items; generally anything that means the **material** world as affected by people.

One can regard *Homo sapiens* as the environmental engineer par excellence, altering whatever his local landscape presents to allow him to live and flourish in the widest variety of climatic zones of any species. Rather than evolve into subspecies with different attributes that provide adaptation to the situation, we change the way we interact, and adapt our tools and the land itself, to provide a fit between Us and Place. By watching animals and their strategies, we have leapfrogged the usual process of biological evolution, our empathy with non-human species allowing us to copy from organisms as if they were our friends and teachers.

Our activities change the face of the planet. No corner remains unaffected, if you have the tools to look with. The remotest location has traces of soot, and other pollutants, dating back thousands of years, laid down from wind carried depositions. The middle of the Pacific and Atlantic oceans hold rafts of plastic detritus, works of Man. We appropriate about 40% of the planet's net primary productivity (i.e., everything that grows). The figures for this vary tremendously, from 10-55%, but pretty much all reliable sources agree on at least a quarter as a reasonable estimate.

And what do we do with this resource? What do we make, move, eat, and build?

I assume that most of us live in surroundings comprised of such structures so, no need to travel especially to the location of these works.

The structure of this week's exercises reflects this, no need for a special journey to search for input as we have in previous weeks.

Instead look at your everyday life, look through memories of your personal role in these processes. Think of soil you have dug, creations you have built, artefacts you have purchased and used (and the origins of these), structures you rely upon each day for your water, transport of yourself and your goods, the building you live in, work in, use in other ways.

Choose a level you feel able to explore, rather than following all trails to the end of their limit, set an arbitrary boundary by whatever criteria you see as meaningful.

If you wish to take this exploration to a species level at some time in the future, you cannot do better than read *Something New Under The Sun: An Environmental History of the Twentieth Century World*. J.R. McNeill, 2001, Norton.

Exercise 1

Throughout your day(s), observe the world as seen through the theme of the Opusphere. Recall your past actions and what you have made of your part of the world.

Exercise 2

Take ten minutes to sit down and write/draw a page of your impressions, in a brainstorm style. Spend ten minutes in meditation upon this list, adding to it as you feel the need to. For now, try not to apply value judgements, keep an objective perspective. Good and bad are like meat and poison, defined by the consumer's reaction rather than any ultimate intrinsic quality.

Exercise 3

After a gap of a day, look at your list again, and now apply your own sense of value to the works you have observed or remembered. Upon reflection, have you lived as you would choose to? Given constraints of availability, could you improve your efficiency of use, and simultaneously improve the pleasure you derive from your world? Find one achievable alteration, and do it. Use magick to assist in this process, create a servitor, charge a sigil, divine what the change could be, etc. Keep this quick and easy.

Banish as often as you feel necessary. Or possibly a bit more often...

NB This week we concentrate solely upon our own modified world. As humans, we have no choice but to see the world as humans do. Next week, the Noosphere, enters the more rarefied world of ideas and concepts, and we may find other creatures' views creeping back in again there, but for this week, we have to have a very self centred attitude.

One aspect of the Opusphere I remain unsure of how to categorise is music. The instruments, the musical notation, clearly fit into the category of material creations, and even the sounds can be interpreted as 'material' effects. However there are also good reasons to include it under the more conceptual frame of the Noosphere... theatre and various other works of Man also fall into a similar across categories realm. Any suggestions as to where you feel they would fit?

Week 4 Noosphere

Frequenters of the information superhighway as we are, the Noosphere appears to us as water to fish. All pervasive, the form of a large part of our identities and social interactions, the source of our inspirations, views of the world, where we disseminate our own ego generated forms into the gaze of other humans.

The other species of our planet contribute to the interweb mediated by human editing. As yet they partake in no way I know of in the active creation or use of cyber information BUT, with the advent of new technological gadgets, their incorporation into digital realms can only be a matter of time.

They do of course have their own access to inputs and outputs of the Noosphere in the physical world, apes to zebras, internal constructs of what to eat, fuck or ignore.

So how do these constructs exist? We know from exhaustive research they have no kind of 'reality' in the brain, and the towards/avoid response of all organisms precedes brains by billions of years.

Information underlies the material existence of the world, yet in our hierarchical placement of information (itself a piece of information!) we tend to have information as the 'top' of our ladder. The GCR puts it as penultimate to the top, with Magick as Higher… however. This results from an artefact of our restricted ability to think only in physical real world 3D form. Our language reflects this internal replication, with object and container words to communicate our ideation of things within. (See Steven Pinker's work if you're interested in learning more on this idea.)

But. Recent examination of the quantum world at the base of our reality ladder, indicates that we live in a physical world that at heart consists of zeroes and ones.

So where does that leave the Noosphere in our created scheme? Well, we leave it where we first placed it; part of our realisation about the magickal world seems to me to have the epiphany of the centrality of the non-hierarchical. In which case we can put it wherever makes most sense to us at that moment, the value for each step on the GCR ladder relies upon itself, not the a b c ordering as having more or less value.

Exercise 1

Working with the Noosphere presents a particular problem, as by our thinking we instantly enter the conceptual. Self reflective observations lead us deeper into the labyrinth. Before entering on an exploration we need to fasten a thread to the outer world. Sit, breathe, feel. Those of you who have practised no thought, enter that state. If not then awareness of the immediate body and breath sensations will do just as well.

From your position, having closed your eyes, imagine yourself rising up, to gain an overview of your mind's architecture. Do you have a two dimensional spread of categories, linked in a network of connections? With places, people, yourself, activities, and abstracts, as the headers of folders within which you place new stimuli; or has it more of the form of hyperlinked text, with each thought form resonating across various categories, depending upon context?

Week 5 Chaosphere

Magick. Use this week to explore you view of Baphomet as a deity. Baphomet, the deity personifying Life on Earth. The egregore of all that lives at this moment.

Just as the Geosphere appears to us as types of rock, the Biosphere as various lifeforms, the Opusphere as diverse forms of handiwork, and the Noosphere as ways of organising our thoughts, the Chaosphere encompasses our individual approaches to magick.

Exercise 1

This week, I'd like us to take a whistle stop tour through our magickal careers to date. Cast a circle, and spend a while going over the first stirrings of interest you had in Magick as a practice, think over the people and places that made it live for you. See those special rituals or moments that sang out with resonance, turned your attention towards the possibilities of reaching beyond the Normal; see the tools you acquired and made, to better engage with the extraordinary world.

This may take some preparatory work going through old diaries, writing out a skeleton plan of the order of things, gathering objects or other resources to prompt vivid memories (favourite incenses of different periods, past pictures of working spaces). The human animal likes physical cues to memory recollection, use this tendency to your advantage.

In particular, trace your personal history of interactions with Baphomet. Revisit, at least in memory if not physically possible, the places where you have encountered strong manifestations of this deity. What triggers the feel for you of Baphomet?

This could take more than one session, so that's the only work for this week!

Week 6 Baphomet invocation

The time has come to invoke! Gather found objects and memes, from any of the previously explored spheres of influence, which evoke for you a feeling of this oldest and youngest of the gods.

Exercise 1

Spend as many days as you like collecting together little (or big!) objects, both physical and from any of the other realms. Note down the thoughts, songs or images that you feel reach out to you. In my experience, the most successful invocations, and indeed rituals, allow for the environment around you to have some input into the personal awareness of the magician.

Sense the Baphometic wider consciousness seeking out You, as a vehicle through which to manifest.

Set a date when you can perform the invocation, giving yourself some space and time for a recovery period. Daytime often works well for Baphomet invocations.

A note of caution; if you haven't taken on a possession state of Baphomet before, sHe tends to like exploring the world so keep doors closed/locked, and dangerous things (e.g. fire, sharp blades) out of reach. Cast your circle with great force to contain the energies! J

Solo possessions rarely result in any major problems, but in group work the intensity of this deity can cause an issue.

Prepare a sacrament for charging with your intent, or an object for consecration.

Keep the intent of any enchantment in keeping with the overall ethos of this particular deity.

After reaching possession, Baphomet often likes to say a few words; try to write these down as soon as possible afterwards before they fade from memory. Or, set up a voice/video recording device prior to the invocation.

Be sure of a successful banishing, as I have mentioned before the standard most effective method is to state your name and address, repeating until you are totally convinced of your individuality once more.

Laugh, like you're never laughed before, and have a small feast awaiting to help ground yourself.

IO BAPHOMET

Fig 15 Baphomet by Lee Noble.

Valediction

From an obscure heretical idol at the heart of crusading Christendom, through the devil of the Masons to the sorcerers' circles of modern witchcraft and wizardry – Baphomet has had a strange journey.

Cut-up deity of fish scales and shaggy legs, of cock and breasts, of eagle wings and raised horns. Icon of Satanists, of Metal fans, of post-modern, post-ironic pop culture.

Glyph of the swirling, inevitable emergence of biological life! Symbol of consciousness embedded in and arising from the world! All-begetter of innumerable forms destined to occupy all n hyperdimensional niches in all existences!

Wide-eyed self-perceiving metaphor, nature looking at itself and understanding itself through itself, through our selves; all-devouring, analysing and self-swallowing awareness. All-destroying impermanence, delighting in vain at the solve et coagula of this Universe.

Funny little goat with wings!

We evoke, celebrate and banish you, with laughter ☺

Selected Bibliography

Barber, Malcolm and Bate, Keith. "The Templars (Manchester Medieval Studies)". Manchester University Press, 2002.

Brighton, Simon. "In Search of the Knights Templar: A Guide to the Sites in Britain". Weidenfeld & Nicolson, 2006.

Campbell, Joseph. "The Masks of God, volumes 1-4". Penguin, 1991.

Carroll, Peter J. "Liber Kaos". Samuel Weiser, 1992.

Carroll, Peter J. "Liber Null and Psychonaut". Red Wheel/Weiser, 1987.

Corazza, Ornella. "Near-Death Experiences: Exploring the Mind-Body Connection". Routledge, 2008.

Crowley, Aleister. "The Book of Lies". Red Wheel/Weiser, 1980.

Crowley, Aleister. "The Book of Thoth". Red Wheel/Weiser, 1981.

Crowley, Aleister. Edited by John Symonds and Kenneth Grant. "Magick". Routledge & Kegan Paul, 1973.

Gardner, Gerald Brosseau. "Meaning of Witchcraft". Aquarian Press, 1976.

Grahame, Kenneth. "The Wind in the Willows". New York: Scribner, 1960.

Grant, Kenneth. "Nightside of Eden". Skoob Esoterica, 1994.

Grey, Peter. "The Red Goddess". Scarlet Imprint, 2007.

Kent, James L. "Psychedelic Information Theory: Shamanism in the Age of Reason". Seattle: PIT Press, 2010.

Laidler, Keith. "The Head Of God: The Lost Treasure of the Templars". Weidenfeld & Nicolson, 1998.

Lane, Nick. "Life Ascending: The Ten Great Inventions of Evolution". Profile Books, 2010.

Lomas, Robert. "The Invisible College". Corgi, 2009.

Lord, Dr Evelyn. "The Knights Templar in Britain". Longman, 2004.

Masters, Robert Augustus. "Darkness Shining Wild: An Odyssey to the Heart of Hell & Beyond: Meditations on Sanity, Suffering, Spirituality, and Liberation". Tehmenos Press, 2005.

Mathews, Freya. "The Ecological Self". London: Routledge, 1993.

McNeill, J.R. "Something New Under the Sun". New York: WW Norton & Company, 2000.

Oroc, James. "Tryptamine Palace: 5-MeO-DMT and the Sonoran Desert Toad: A Journey from Burning Man to the Akashic Field". Inner Traditions / Park Street Press, 2009.

Partner, Peter. "The Knights Templar and Their Myth". Inner Traditions Bear and Company, 1990.

Pinker, Steven. "The Stuff of Thought: Language as a Window into Human Nature". Penguin, 2008.

Shea, R. and Wilson, R.A. "The Illuminatus! Trilogy". London: Dell Publishing, 1975.

Shulgin, Alexander, Shulgin, Ann and Joy, Dan. "Tihkal: The Continuation". Transform Press, 1997.

Turner, Fred. "From Counterculture to Cyberculture: Stewart Brand, the Whole Earth Network and the Rise of Digital Utopianism". University of Chicago Press, 2006.

Valiente, Doreen. "Witchcraft for Tomorrow". Robert Hale, 1978.

What is allotted truth, entirely, is not

nothing is, everything permission had applicable

nothing is not genuine, all is allowed

nothing is to align, all is concurred

Anything truth does, is permitted

Anything is not real, all are permitted

nothing n' is true, all is authorized

nothing is allowed is truth, everything

Nichts ist wahr alles ist erlaubt

Nothing is true everything is permitted

Нищо вярно, всичко позволено

Ag I Hoath; Tofglo I Dlugam

Nix is fix, Ois is möglich

Nix is woa, Ois is erlaubt

ничего истинно, все позволено

Nüt esch wohr, alles esch erlaubt

Nic nie je pravda, vsetko je dovolene

Chacuchad Vonzog: Chipuvt Tehacfa!

Niente è vero, tutto è conceduto!

Nada é verdadeiro. Tudo é Permitido

Nada es verdad. Todo está permitido

Does dim byd yn wir, mae popeth yn bosib

rien n'est vrai, tout est permis

لا شيء ثابت...كل شيء مباح

Nenio estas Vera - Chio estas Permesita

Ingenting er sant, alt er lov

Inget är sant, allting är tillåtet

没什么是真的，什么都成。

Nic není pravda, v'echno je dovoleno.

Semmi se igaz, minden meg van engedve.

Nothing is static, everything is evolving.

It's all bullshit. Just pick something

Whatever man, it's all good

Fuck it, let's do this shit

Nothing is true unless it was properly documented; anything is permitted as long as you don't get caught.

Everything is permitted as long as you're a hard-working W.A.S.P

Its not proper tidy truth see, its all over the shop mon, but it is proper tidy to do as you will see

Todo es verdad, mañana es otro día!

Alles ist wahr, morgen sehen wir mal.

Nothing is fixed, everything is mutable

Everything is true, tomorrow is another day.

Tenemos leyes muy estrictas pero a nadie le importa!

Wir haben strenge Gesetze, keiner kümmert sich darum.

We have strict laws, no-one cares.

Nada se puede hacer pero todo es posible!

Nix geht hier, trotzdem ist alles möglich.

Nothing works here, but everything is possible.

Nothing is fattening. All is delicious!

nothing is absolute, everything is relative

Nothing has absolute truth, anything may prove possible

Mandrake
'Books you don't see everyday'

The Apophenion: A Chaos Magic Paradigm by Peter J Carroll

978-1869928-421, £10.99

My final Magnum Opus if its ideas remain unfalsified within my lifetime, otherwise its back to the drawing board. Yet I've tried to keep it as short and simple as possible, it consists of eight fairly brief and terse chapters and five appendices.

It attacks most of the great questions of being, free will, consciousness, meaning, the nature of mind, and humanity's place in the cosmos, from a magical perspective. Some of the conclusions seem to challenge many of the deeply held assumptions that our culture has taught us, so brace yourself for the paradigm crash and look for the jewels revealed in the wreckage.

This book contains something to offend everyone; enough science to upset the magicians, enough magic to upset the scientists, and enough blasphemy to upset most trancendentalists.

The most original, and probably the most important, writer on Magick since Aleister Crowley.
        -Robert Anton Wilson, author of the *Cosmic Trigger* trilogy.

Bright From the Well by Dave Lee

978-1869928-841, £10.99

'Bright From the Well' consists of five stories plus five essays and a rune-poem. The stories revolve around themes from Norse myth - the marriage of Frey and Gerd, the story of how Gullveig-Heidh reveals her powers to the gods, a modern take on the social-origins myth Rig's Tale, Loki attending a pagan pub moot and the Ragnarok seen through the eyes of an ancient shaman.

The essays include examination of the Norse creation or origins story, of the magician in or against the world and a chaoist's magical experiences looked at from the standpoint of Northern magic.'

'Dave Lee coaches breathwork, writes fiction and non-fiction, blends incenses and oils, creates music and collages'

Magick Works: cutting edge essays from the path of Pleasure, Freedom and Power by Julian Vayne

978-1869928-469 £10.99

Enter the world of the occultist: where the spirits of the dead dwell amongst us, where the politics of ecstasy are played out, and where magick spills into every aspect of life.

It's all right here; sex, drugs, witchcraft and gardening. From academic papers, through to first person accounts of high-octaine rituals. In Magick Works you will find cutting edge essays from the path of Pleasure, Freedom and Power.

In this seminal collection Julian Vayne explores;

* The Tantric use of Ketamine.
* Social Justice, Green Politics and Druidry.
* English Witchcraft and Macumba
* The Magickal use of Space.
* Cognitive Liberty and the Occult.
* Psychogeography & Chaos Magick.
* Tai Chi and Apocalyptic Paranoia.
* Self-identity, Extropianism and the Abyss.
* Parenthood as Spiritual Practice.
* Aleister Crowley as Shaman

...and much more!

Other Mandrake Titles:

Fries/*Cauldron of the Gods: a manual of Celtic Magick.* 552pp, royal octavo, 9781869928612 £24.99$40 paper

Fries/*Seidways Shaking, Swaying and Serpent Mysteries.* 350pp 9781869928360 £15/$25
Still the definitive and much sought after study of magical trance and possession techniques.

Fries/*Helrunar - a manual of rune magick.* 454pp 9781968828902 pbk, £19.99/$40 Over 130 illustrations. new enlarged and improved edition
'...eminently practical and certainly breaks new ground.' - Ronald Hutton

Order direct from

Mandrake of Oxford

PO Box 250, Oxford, OX1 1AP (UK)

Phone: 01865 243671

(for credit card sales)

Prices include economy postage

Visit our web site

online at - www.mandrake.uk.net